Young Writers 2005 POE

PLAYGROUND

Let your creativity flow...

ode

limerick haiku

rhyme

Scotland
Edited by Aimée Vanstone

Young**Writers**

First published in Great Britain in 2005 by:
Young Writers
Remus House
Coltsfoot Drive
Peterborough
PE2 9JX
Telephone: 01733 890066
Website: www.youngwriters.co.uk

SB ISBN 1 84602 104 9

Foreword

Young Writers was established in 1991 and has been passionately devoted to the promotion of reading and writing in children and young adults ever since. The quest continues today. Young Writers remains as committed to the fostering of burgeoning poetic and literary talent as ever.

This year's Young Writers competition has proven as vibrant and dynamic as ever and we are delighted to present a showcase of the best poetry from across the UK. Each poem has been carefully selected from a wealth of *Playground Poets* entries before ultimately being published in this, our thirteenth primary school poetry series.

Once again, we have been supremely impressed by the overall high quality of the entries we have received. The imagination, energy and creativity which has gone into each young writer's entry made choosing the best poems a challenging and often difficult but ultimately hugely rewarding task - the general high standard of the work submitted amply vindicating this opportunity to bring their poetry to a larger appreciative audience.

We sincerely hope you are pleased with our final selection and that you will enjoy *Playground Poets Scotland* for many years to come.

Contents

Michael Low (10)   15
James McMillan (9)   15
Andrew Miller (9)   15
Danielle Moran (9)   16
Alistair John Campbell Nairn (8)   16
Puravi Kumar (9)   16
Katie McDonald (9)   17
Heather McDevitt (9)   17
Samantha Potter (8)   17
Freyja Wilson (10)   18
Rebecca Mayer (9)   19
Rachel Henderson (9)   20
Elliot Provan (9)   20
Grant Perston (10)   20
John Morley (10)   21
Grant Cairney (10)   21
Lisa Summers (10)   21
Callum Stewart (10)   22
Lindsay Robertson (10)   22
Jonathan Elliott (10)   23
Michael Abrami (10)   23
Andrew Cuthbert (10)   24
Stuart Wiseman (9)   25
Ananya Kokkranikal (10)   25
Craig Imrie (10)   25
Stuart Taylor (10)   26
Calum Husenne (10)   26
Catriona McCallum (10)   27
Jamie Meldrum (10)   27
Euan Waugh (10)   28

Conon Bridge Primary School, Dingwall
Sunita Schrijvers (8)   28
Rachel McKay (7)   28
Jack Cuthbertson (7)   29
Christopher Urquhart (7)   29
Robert McAllister (7)   29
Michael Gillett (7)   30
Stephen Greenhowe (7)   30
Kieran McSwegan (7)   30
Bethany Skidmore (6)   31

Andrew Forsyth (7)   31
Scott McLaughlin (7)   31

Finzean School, Banchory

Lyndsey Gordon (7)   32
Katie Thow (7)   32
Donna Winton (7)   32
Emma Lawson (7)   32
Euan Christie (7)   33
Josephine Christie (8)   33
Alistair Winton (8)   33
Neil Thomson-Mitchell (8)   33
Marianne Mackie (8)   34
Jodie Maher (8)   34
Erin Lloyd (8)   34

Head of Muir Primary School, Denny

Emma Baillie (7)   34
Dayna Leckie (7)   35
Alasdair Pemble (7)   35
Ross Weir (7)   35
Daniel MacFarlane (7)   36
Sophie Rawding (7)   36
Chloe White (6)   36
John Campbell (7)   36
Iain Crossan (7)   37
David Cunningham (7)   37
Ruth Dyson (7)   37
Eilidh Ferguson (7)   37
Blair Forbes (7)   38
Ross Gray (7)   38
Kirsten Harrower (7)   38
Kiranjeet Kaur (7)   38
Connor Mitchell (11)   39
Jill Hunter (11)   39
Scott Shanks (10)   40
Alana Galbraith (10)   40
Eve Whitelaw (11)   41
Jenna Douglas (7)   41

Kincardine-in-Menteith Primary School, Stirling

Teddi Anderson (10)   42
Sean McBeath (8)   42
James McBeath (11)   43
Phil Aitken (9)   43
Amanda Killen (10)   44

Kippen Primary School, Stirling

Struan Scott (11)   45
Maura Collins (11)   46
Robert Kilpatrick (11)   47
Daniel McBride (11)   48
Beth Finlay (11)   49
Jack Turner (11)   49

Kirklandpark Primary School, Strathaven

Ethan Carle (11)   50
Gregor Stirling (10)   51
Daniel Harris (10)   52
Martha Smart (11)   53
Jessica Duff (10)   54
Euan Paterson (11)   55
Ellie Lee (11)   56
Georgia McKay (11)   57
Karen Adamson (11)   58
Amy Sterritt (11)   59
Alistair Coull (11)   60

Leith Walk Primary School, Edinburgh

Melanie Murray (10)   60
Tammy Walker (10)   61
Jack Shearer (10)   62
Lipa Hussain (10)   63

Lismore Primary School, Argyll

Murray Willis (11)   63
Joe Derham (11)   64
Eilidh Willis (9)   64
John Carmichael (9)   64

Calum McGillivray (10)   65
Keiran McLarney (11)   65
Emma Sanderson (9)   66

Marybank Primary School, Muir of Ord
Alannah Warner (9)   66
Jessica Dean (9)   67
Andrew Brown (9)   67
Zoe Thorpe (9)   67
Emily Brydon (9)   68
Louise Muirhead (8)   68
Marsaili Stewart-Skinner (9)   69

Meadowburn Primary School, Bishopbriggs
Lynn Smith (9)   69
Eilidh Munro (11)   70
Heather Kindness (10)   71
Jamie Murray (10)   72
James Morrison (9)   72
Fraser Munro (9)   73
Ishbal MacLennan (10)   74
Hannah Macintosh (9)   75

Muirtown Primary School, Inverness
Bruce Gibson (10)   75
Ethan Turner (9)   76
Aiden Lyall (9)   76
Caitlin MacColl (9)   77
Hazel Blackhall (9)   77
Graeme Goddard (9)   78
Ellie Munro (9)   78
Amy Anderson (9)   78
Erin Wardlaw (9)   79
Anna Bown (9)   79
Bobby Chisholm (9)   80
Kieran Macgillivray (9)   80
Liam Macleod (9)   81
Avie Sutherland (9)   81
Rhuary MacDougall (10)   82

Ciara Polson (9) 82
Connor Munro (10) 82
Morven Macdonald (9) 83

Our Lady of Peace Primary School, Paisley
Kerri Whyte (10) 83
Paul Flannigan (10) 83
Frankie Barrett (10) 84
Kelly-Anne McDougall (10) 84
Emma Cunningham (10) 84
Ellese McInalty (10) 85
Kerry Docherty (10) 85
Shona Strachan (10) 85
Chloe Gorton (10) 86
Seona Kelly (10) 86

Port Elphinstone Primary School, Inverurie
Sarah Smith (10) 87
Laura Jaffray (8) 87
Rachel Murray (9) 88
Dean Sockalingum (9) 88
Lauren McGhee (10) 89
Jamie Fenty (9) 89
Matthew Gillies (8) 90
Nadia Warner (8) 90
Melissa Morrice (9) 90
William Mutch (10) 91

Ravenswood Primary School, Cumbernauld
Gary Pullar (11) 91
Lori-Jaye Hooks (11) 91
Adam Jenkins (11) 92
Amy Allan (11) 92
Alastair Stephen (12) 93
Christopher Reid (11) 93
Louise Donaldson (11) 93
Hollie Lang (11) 94
Scott Girvan (11) 94
Chloe Rice (11) 94

Stefan Weir (11)	95
Amy Lightfoot (11)	95
Jennifer Ward (11)	95
Rebecca Redmond (11)	96
David McMeeking (11)	96
Danielle Hall (11)	96
Rebecca Taylor (11)	97
Ryan Hendrie (11)	97
Heather Speedie (11)	97
Mark Adams (11)	98
Gavin Rae (11)	98
Steven Harvie (11)	98
Michael Stewart (11)	99

St Leonards School, St Andrews

Janet Mary Provan (8)	99
Oliver Rogers-Jones (8)	100
Oliver de Mountfalcon (9)	100
Jonathan Blackburn (9)	100
Robert Clark (10)	101
Callum Morse (8)	101
Bethany Ferguson (8)	102
Elizabeth Clark (8)	102
Andrew Taylor (9)	103
Rebecca Mackay (8)	103
Olivia Gibson (9)	104
Oliver Hazell (9)	104
Jordan Hutchison (8)	105
David Mackay (9)	105
Holly Milne (9)	106
Nina Duncan (9)	106
Katie Overend (9)	107
Hannah Gray (9)	107
Richard Ward (10)	108
Jaimie Morse (9)	108
Ged Rutherford (10)	109
Tabitha Gordon-Smith (8)	109
Jasmine Wilson (10)	110
Keir Hunter (9)	110
Rebecca Taylor (10)	111

Cameron Spencer (10)   112
Flora Ogilvy (10)   113
Emilie Chalmers (11)   113
Adam Harris (11)   114
Josh Jamieson (11)   114
Alice Ferguson (11)   115

St Mary's Primary School, Maryhill
Nicolle Briggs (11)   116
Alexander McIntosh (11)   116
Danielle Brown (11)   116
Leanne Monaghan (11)   117
Shelley Burke & Eilidh MacNeill (10)   117
Kerry Spence (11)   117
Lauren Grieve (11)   118

St Peter's RC Primary School, Aberdeen
Kieran Wilkie (8)   118
Toni-Marie Wharry (8)   119
Dario Giuseppe Piedipalumbo (8)   119
Bronach Boyle (8)   120
Jaime Robb (8)   121
Parham Tadayon (8)   122
Lauren Baxter (9)   122
Eden Johnson (8)   123
Chipego Siamuwele (8)   123
Shannen Katerina Romero-Pérez (8)   124
Matthew Ross (8)   124
Jack Alexander (8)   125
Shalin Abraham (8)   125
Nicole Anderson (8)   126
Clyde Hoskin (9)   127

Tanshall Primary School, Glenrothes
Hayley Lynch (10)   127
Ashleigh Curtis (10)   128
Liam Baxter (10)   128
Ryan Hutton (10)   128
Kayleigh Finlay (9)   129

Stacey Gell (11) 129
Stacey Knox (11) 130
Ryan Watson (10) 130
Nadia Mohammed (10) 131
Steven Neil (10) 131
Philip Gibson (11) 131
Thomas Lowe (10) 132
Martin Foy (12) 132
Ryan Kelly (10) 132

Westhill Primary School, Westhill

Rachel Paterson & Eilidh Bett (11) 133
Euan Dodds & Scott Milne (11) 133
Ben Little (11) 133
Murray Cruickshank, Diane Fowler & Magnus Warr (11) ... 134
Euan Duthie & Chris Kerr (11) 134
Stephanie Clarke & Rona Parkinson (11) 135
Kirsty MacNeil (11) 135
Jenna Hendry & Kirsty Ogston 135
Cameron Burgess (10) & Abbie Fleming (11) 136
Natalie Rowley (11) 136
Laurie Stuart (11) 136
Calum Ritchie & Alastair Forsyth (11) 137
Amber Wynn & Nicole Anderson (10) 137
Jack Davidson & Elliott Pettitt (11) 137
Molly Bedrock & Tabatha Wright (10) 138
Paul Sheach, Jinu Jang & Sean Cowie (10) 138
Ailsa Collie & Nia McKain 138
Zakary Rothwell & Gillian Wright (10) 139
David Ross Mackenzie & Kyle Johannesson (11) 139
Stephanie Allard & Jack Grimmer (11) 139
Graham Repper (10) 140
Kirsty Gollifer (10) & Johanna Goldie (11) 140
Stuart Duncan (11) 140

Woodlands Primary School, Irvine

Jordan Stevely (11) 141
Ruth Dempster (8) 141
Katie Bell (11) 142
Ashley Donaghy (8) 142

The Poems

Endangered Animals

I am angry about the hunters
Killing the baby seals.
You might think that they end up being somebody's meals,
Well here's a surprise for you, you're wrong!
They end up as a lady's purse, nice, furry and long.

Think about the poor little pups ending up as something like that
Maybe a purse, maybe a bag or a beautiful lady's hat.
I really want to help the pups, I do, I do, I do!
So I'm going to join the WWF and see if that will help too.
I want to help to save that pup's rights
Because I won't give up without a fight.

Laura Foy (9)
Bonhill Primary School, Alexandria

Seal Pup

I was sitting beside my mum
Just then I saw a terrible sight
A hunter was coming to get me
I could not do anything
My mum was asleep,
I started to howl.
Suddenly, I felt something on my head.
I struggled and struggled to get away.
But it was too late,
I was dead.

Sarah Brodie (8)
Bonhill Primary School, Alexandria

Whale

I am a whale lover
I think that the hunters are sad.
I think that the whales will cry at night for their life.
I know why they kill the whales for money.
At night when I lie in my bed I think of them and how they get killed.
When I was walking along the beach I saw a whale
It looked at me with fear.
I think I know why the hunters kill them
It is for make-up and polish.
Now I think there will soon be no whales left.

Tiffany Chisholm (9)
Bonhill Primary School, Alexandria

Recycling

We're recycling
so what can be reused?
Tins and cans
there's so many to choose.
Whatever you put in
is always used again.
We like recycling
so you will too,
so put something in
and see what you can do.
Make the rubbish vanish
without a trace
and turn this world
into a better place.

Chloe da Costa (9)
Bonhill Primary School, Alexandria

Recycle, Recycle

Yo, yo, yo give me some glass,
So we can recycle it into cash!
Plastic is fantastic,
Give me some elastic,
Even something drastic
Like tin, tin, tin.

Eve Tuckwood (9)
Bonhill Primary School, Alexandria

My Mum

Her eyes are like diamonds
Her smile is so bright
Her writing is so neat
Her clothes are so nice
But the best thing is
She is my mum
And she loves me!

Louise Gardiner (9)
Bonhill Primary School, Alexandria

Off Road Buggy

Sunday morning, jump and grab the keys on the way outside.
Open the garage, pull the buggy outside.
Jumping into the seat, pulling the trailer out from the big grass heap.
Get to the track and there's Sandy in his little Mini.
He asks me for a race along the big grass straight.
We're waiting at the starting line, ready to go,
Press the pedal right down to the metal.
I am coming to the finish line and Sandy's still chugging
along behind . . .

Grant Bowman (11)
Carmichael Primary School, Biggar

My Nephew Ben

My nephew Ben
Steals my stuff
And is really rough,
He punches me
And kicks me,
Sometimes he even licks me . . .

Although sometimes he's OK
When we go out to play,
But he still hurts me
And says that I'm ugly,
Still, he's only 3,
Soon he'll be nicer to me.

Kate Macauley (10)
Carmichael Primary School, Biggar

Fitbaw

I want to play fitbaw
Ma mammy keeps sayin' naw.
'Tidy that room o' yours!
It smells like somethin' oot the sewers!'
'I dinna want tae tidy me room.'
'You tidy that room and use that broom!'
'But I want to go oot on the playgrun'!'
'No buts son, you get your room tidy or nay fun!'
I keep on nagging my maw to go and play
But it seems it disna' matter whit a say!

Jamie Telfer (11)
Carmichael Primary School, Biggar

My Cousin

My cousin Carly is a pain
She loves playing in the rain
Carly likes ballet
And watches the rally
And says that her mum is a train.

She slides down the chute
Turns the telly to mute
Goes down to town
She likes the colour brown
Sometimes she is very cute.

Alistair Scott (10)
Carmichael Primary School, Biggar

My Idols

My mum and dad are my idols
Yes my idols
My birthday is coming soon
Usually I choose what I want to do
Mum said she'll choose this year
And she said, I'm not having a party
No, she does not give in.
Dad on the other hand,
Dad would let me do anything
All I have to do is smile
Dad's a softy underneath!

Alice Nisbet (9)
Carmichael Primary School, Biggar

Fightin' For Britain

A want to be a fighter pilot.
Mama says, 'You'll be dead within the week knowin' you.'
But I ken that I'll be a pilot
I can just picture ma sel,
In that cockpit, fightin' for Britain.

Sandy Mitchell (9)
Carmichael Primary School, Biggar

Rosie

R osie is my little sister
O ver the moon all of the time
S inging along to her favourite songs
 I must confess she's a bit of a pest
E ven though I love her to bits.

Penelope Jack (9)
Carmichael Primary School, Biggar

The Rock

T errifying and strong
H e'll break all their bones
E ntertaining and cool

R ock's coming to town
O rdinary he is not
C oming to fight Big Show
K nockout Big Show.

Ross Meikle (9)
Carmichael Primary School, Biggar

Happiness

Happiness is yellow.
Happiness smells like a baby daffodil lighting up the garden
And tastes like a big, juicy pineapple.
Happiness looks like a lioness feeding its young
And sounds like a bluebird tweeting in the distance.
Happiness is being with your family.

David Shearer (8)
Carolside Primary School, Clarkston

Happiness

Happiness is blue.
Happiness smells like lovely bright roses
And tastes like a Crunchie covered in lovely dark chocolate.
Happiness looks like children playing in the snow
And sounds like adults laughing.
Happiness is when Scotland win the World Cup.

Gregor McInnes (8)
Carolside Primary School, Clarkston

Happiness

Happiness is sunny yellow.
Happiness smells like a triple sponge chocolate cake
And tastes like a giant pepperoni pizza.
Happiness looks like a candy cane growing and growing
And sounds like a peaceful breeze before sunset.
Happiness is playing with your friends.

Michael Goldberg (8)
Carolside Primary School, Clarkston

Happiness

Happiness is blue.
Happiness smells like pretty flowers in the light blue sky.
Happiness tastes like the strong smell of Polo Mints.
Happiness looks like people playing in the snow on a cold,
                                        wintry morning.
Happiness sounds like people singing in a choir.
Happiness is with my family.

Matthew Kirkwood (8)
Carolside Primary School, Clarkston

Fear

Fear is black.
Fear smells like rotten wood from a door and tastes like fresh blood.
Fear looks like shadows creeping around a room
And sounds like a door slamming after you.
Fear is not having a family.

Adam Taylor (8)
Carolside Primary School, Clarkston

Anger

Anger is red.
Anger smells like rotten vegetables
And tastes like horrible medicine.
Anger looks like cars crashing
And sounds like a woman screaming.
Anger is smoke coming out of my ears.

Katie Brydie (8)
Carolside Primary School, Clarkston

Death

(In memory of all who died in the tsunami)

A dark, black, hooded cloak,
And scythe with handle made of oak,
No head, expression, thoughts or face,
No body, arms, legs, not a trace.
Just cold air inside a pitch-black sheet,
No eyes, no ears, no mouth, no feet.

He quickly and quietly stalks his victim,
Lying in wait for the chance to strike him,
The triumphant king of death is he,
As he hears his victim's frightened plea.
He does the deed, not a care in the world,
Of leaving a body lifeless, mangled and gnarled.

Melissa McNair (9)
Carolside Primary School, Clarkston

Tsunami Trauma

After the biggest trauma of the year,
A traumatised father still searches here,
Crawling in the rubble,
Searching, searching, such a struggle.

What's this? A figure?
Small and weak,
His son at last but alas! No pulse,
Not a breath was heard, not a word was said.

Until this day he searches,
With hope dimming,
Like a cave of misery,
On the darkest night of the year.

Rachel McGarvey (9)
Carolside Primary School, Clarkston

Bad Girl Sophie

'Sophie, Sophie, what have you done?
You're meant to be a nun.'
'I didn't mean to hurt you by far,
All I did was vandalise your car.'

'Sophie, Sophie, what have you done?
You're meant to be a nun.'
'Sorry, Mr Pie
I didn't mean to cut your tie.'

'Sophie, Sophie, what have you done?
You're meant to be a nun.'
'Sorry I knocked you off your seat,
But I wanted to be comfortable watching Coronation Street.'

'Sophie, Sophie what have you done?
You're meant to be a nun.'
'Sorry I sneezed on your shoe,
But I've got the flu.'

'Sophie, Sophie what have you done?
You're meant to be a nun.'
'Sorry for all the things I've done,
I just wanted to prove I'm not a nun.'

Lauren McLemon (10)
Carolside Primary School, Clarkston

Underwater

Splash you're underwater,
You don't know where you're going,
You only know you're flowing,
You go up once but come down again,
You go up again,
But sink till you're dead.

Euan McGowan (9)
Carolside Primary School, Clarkston

Tsunami Destruction

Scary, big and drowning,
Rubble, dark.
I can't see a thing,
Blood-red death
Is what I'm about to suffer,
Petrified and lost
From my family.
What destruction tsunamis can cause,
Searching for homeland,
Lost in deep blue sea,
Can't breathe, help me.

Blair Mackie (9)
Carolside Primary School, Clarkston

Death

Death is like a shadow
That will never stop haunting you,
Death is like a big black cloud
With thunder everywhere,
A loaf of bread is like steel or lead,
And all the trees are dead and bare.

The tsunami was a shock to me,
I'm sure everyone would have wanted to flee,
Everyone dying, everyone in sight,
What a terrible night!

Shona McHugh (9)
Carolside Primary School, Clarkston

Death

Sad to say they passed away,
How bad could it have been?
It would have been terrifying if you'd seen it,
It would've been terrifying to see bit by bit being damaged,
People still looking for bodies,
Please give money for the tsunami.

Kyle Graham (9)
Carolside Primary School, Clarkston

Tsunami

Water rises and floods expand
Through the road that turns like an elastic band,
Through that country that was so grand
Through that country that looked like a band.
The water that rises and floods the turning road,
What was it? It was the tsunami.

Craig Young (9)
Carolside Primary School, Clarkston

Tsunami

Ten double decker buses,
On top of each other,
Cutting through the water,
Free with no bother,
Fifty lorries at full speed,
Taking lives with immense greed,
People fleeing left and right,
Families lost and out of sight.

Iain McClenaghan (9)
Carolside Primary School, Clarkston

My Doll

I used to have a doll
She had curly, blonde hair,
And big blue eyes that always seemed to stare.

She had shiny white shoes,
And a little tartan dress,
And a red hair ribbon,
That was a terrible mess.

She had a tiny white face,
With ruby-red lips,
And charcoal-black eyelashes,
That curled up to the tips.

She was really, really lovely,
My favourite ever doll,
I used to take her everywhere,
Even to the football!

Aimee McKinven (10)
Carolside Primary School, Clarkston

Reflections And Shadows

A reflection is a strange thing,
It's like another you,
If you smile at something,
It will smile too.

But if you move away,
It cannot be found,
And all you have for company,
Is a shadow on the ground.

Karen Barclay (10)
Carolside Primary School, Clarkston

Death

Death is like cold water,
Icy and sore,
Death is like the tax man,
Knocking on your door.

Death is black like night-time,
You will not see it come,
It tastes sour like a lemon,
But there is hope for some.

Death looks like a knife,
Piercing and sharp,
Death sounds like a high-pitched scream,
Nothing like a lovely harp.

So make the most of your life,
Have fun, help people too,
For one day when you're very old,
Death will come for you.

Laura McAughtrie (10)
Carolside Primary School, Clarkston

Chocolate

C hocolate chip cookies crumbling in my mouth,
H ot chocolate swirling around in my mug,
O range crispy bits smothered in the stuff,
C reamy, smooth, dreamy, silk chocolate,
O -shaped balls of malt,
L uxurious mixture presented in a box,
A ll sorts of shapes, sizes and colours,
T emptation too hard to resist,
E njoy (and don't think of the calories!)

Christopher Anderson (10)
Carolside Primary School, Clarkston

Haunted

H owling wolves cry
A nd so does the wind
U nder the cellar you can
N early feel
T he bats'
E very move, until
D awn strikes.

Michael Low (10)
Carolside Primary School, Clarkston

War

War is black,
It smells like smoke,
War's taste would make you choke,
War sounds like cracking,
War is pain,
War lives down the drain.

James McMillan (9)
Carolside Primary School, Clarkston

Hope

Hope is bright yellow,
It smells like tender chicken,
Hope tastes like chocolate cake,
It sounds like church bells ringing,
It feels warm inside,
Hope comes from the spirit.

Andrew Miller (9)
Carolside Primary School, Clarkston

Happiness

Happiness is bright,
It smells of a daffodil,
It tastes like yummy chocolate,
It sounds like birds singing,
It feels like you're touching cotton wool,
Happiness lives in your heart.

Danielle Moran (9)
Carolside Primary School, Clarkston

Untitled

War is pitch-black,
It smells like thick smoke,
It tastes like blood,
It sounds like banging balloons,
It feels very painful,
War lives in Hell.

Alistair John Campbell Nairn (8)
Carolside Primary School, Clarkston

Happiness

Happiness is green,
It smells like daisies,
Happiness tastes like creamy Swiss rolls,
It sounds like birds singing,
It feels safe and cuddly,
Happiness lives in your heart.

Puravi Kumar (9)
Carolside Primary School, Clarkston

War

War is red with black stripes on it,
War smells like a smoky fire,
War tastes like burnt chips,
War sounds like jets zooming by,
War feels like being locked in a dark cupboard,
War lives down the scary lane.

Katie McDonald (9)
Carolside Primary School, Clarkston

Sadness

Sadness is grey,
It smells like an old shoe,
It tastes like a rotten cabbage,
It sounds like a squeaky shoe,
It feels as heavy as a wall,
And it lives in the drain.

Heather McDevitt (9)
Carolside Primary School, Clarkston

Hope

Hope is bright yellow,
It smells like toasted marshmallows,
It tastes like candy,
Hope sounds like the birds singing,
It feels very soft,
Hope lives in your heart.

Samantha Potter (8)
Carolside Primary School, Clarkston

Under The Sea

Let's go under the water,
To see what we can see,
North or South Pacific,
Which one shall it be?

Let's go to one near Australia,
To see some wonderful fish,
Now let's go to Sydney,
We're almost there, you can hear the water swish.

Jump, jump in now,
It's alright, you can breathe,
And please be quiet,
I don't want the fish to leave.

Oh, look a ray and a squid,
And a clownfish who says 'Boo!'
An eel, a sea horse,
I can see a *shark too!*

Quick, quick, run away,
Or should that be swim?
Just get away from it,
Before we lose every limb.

Quick get on the boat,
We're safe now,
We got away so fast,
I really wonder how.

Freyja Wilson (10)
Carolside Primary School, Clarkston

The Train

Waiting on the platform,
The train is very warm,
The people go on,
The people go on,
The people wave,
As the train goes into the cave,
Off it goes,
Off it goes,
People are talking,
As the train is locking,
Tickets please,
Tickets please,
Put on your belts,
As the coal melts,
The train is going,
The train is going,
The train is fast,
Nearly there at last,
Nearly there,
Nearly there,
The train stops,
People look at the clock,
We're on time!
We're on time!

Rebecca Mayer (9)
Carolside Primary School, Clarkston

Being Afraid

Being afraid is . . .
Breaking your arm, running away from a dog on holiday,
Going to the hospital,
Having a cat scratch you,
When I had to take the bin out when it was dark,
Being left alone in my car,
Going to bed on my own,
When the funfair man spun me fast in a spinning teacup.

Rachel Henderson (9)
Carolside Primary School, Clarkston

Fear

Fear is dark blue,
It smells like a rotten shoe,
It tastes like sweet mango,
It sounds like kids doing the tango!
It feels like a black heart,
Living in horrible strawberry tarts!

Elliot Provan (9)
Carolside Primary School, Clarkston

Cheetahs

C heetahs are very big cats,
H ave very sharp teeth to suffocate their victim,
E at very quickly so other animals can't steal it,
E ating is vital, if they don't they will starve to death,
T hey are the fastest land animal in the world,
A nd have sharp claws for scratching,
H ave a powerful strike to make sure there is
                            no escape for their victim.

Grant Perston (10)
Carolside Primary School, Clarkston

Dinosaur, Dinosaur

I once had a dinosaur who lived under my bed,
I once had a dinosaur whose first name was Ted,
I once had a dinosaur who had a big head,
I once had a dinosaur who just wants some bread,
I once had a dinosaur who had a bear called Fred.

But now he is gone, who knows where?
But some day he will come back and just stare,
All I know is he left his bear!

John Morley (10)
Carolside Primary School, Clarkston

Happiness

Happiness is like a soft cloud floating in the sky,
Happiness is yellow like the sun and will never go dark,
Happiness is smooth, soft, not rough and has no corners,
Happiness is always relaxed, no shouting, tears or anger,
Happiness gently cuddles its prey,
Happiness will never go away and I know I'm happy.

Grant Cairney (10)
Carolside Primary School, Clarkston

Hamsters

H airy, happy,
A mazing,
M onkeys,
S ick when they eat human food,
T iptoeing, turning,
E njoyable, energetic,
R unning like a cheetah,
S pinning 100 miles per minute on their wheel!

Lisa Summers (10)
Carolside Primary School, Clarkston

Malteser Monster

Around the city the Malteser monster would cry,
'I want Maltesers, Malteser's juice or Malteser pie!'

There he stood,
Two hundred feet tall,
Nobody tried to stop him,
Nobody at all.

He rolled into a building,
He ran through the town,
He glared at everyone,
So big and so brown.

Along came a boy,
As small as a fox,
And said, 'OK monster,
Get back in the box!'

Callum Stewart (10)
Carolside Primary School, Clarkston

Favourite Things

These are some of my favourite things . . .

I like dragons because they can fly way up in the sky,
They can blow fire red-hot and steamy.

I like going to the fair,
I just have to stop for a stare,
I like the rides and getting candyfloss.

I like animals,
How the elephant calls,
How the giraffes have such a long neck,
And the cheetahs run so fast.

Lindsay Robertson (10)
Carolside Primary School, Clarkston

You Have It, They Don't

You walk for miles but is it worth it?
You go somewhere and it's closed,
Then you hike and that's boring,
Some people have to walk miles for
Food and water, is that worth it?
So you think you're not lucky!
But if you have a warm house
And loving family,
That's all you need.
Some people, even thousands,
Have nothing, not even their family
So how would you like that?

Jonathan Elliott (10)
Carolside Primary School, Clarkston

My Dad

My dad is silly,
My dad is strong,
My dad is funny,
When he goes wrong.

My dad goes hiking,
My dad goes running,
My dad goes drumming,
It really sounds like he's humming.

My dad plays golf,
My dad plays football,
My dad plays hockey,
He really plays like a donkey,
But whatever he does,
He's still the best dad ever.

Michael Abrami (10)
Carolside Primary School, Clarkston

I'm Hungry

'Hey Fiona,' I said to my sister one day,
'Can you get me something to eat,
A small piece of chicken, or any kind of meat?'
'No go away,' she said,
'Leave me alone,
I'm sitting here talking on the phone.'

'Hey Susan,' I said, 'can you get me something to eat,
A small piece of chicken, or any kind of meat?'
'No,' she said, 'you ask every week,
It's just attention you're trying to seek.'

'Hey Mum,' I said, 'can you get me something to eat,
A small piece of chicken or any kind of meat?'
'No,' she said, 'don't bother me,
I'm working here, can't you see?'

'Hey Dad,' I said, 'can you get me something to eat,
A small piece of chicken, or any kind of meat?'
'Andrew, Andrew,' he said, 'don't be bad,
Andrew, Andrew don't make me mad!'

'Oh be quiet,' my family said,
'Or we'll send you to your bed!'
'If you don't go up those stairs,
We will feed you to the bears!'

'If you don't get me some food,
I think I'll go in a horrible mood!
If you don't get me something to eat,
I will show my stinky feet!'

Andrew Cuthbert (10)
Carolside Primary School, Clarkston

Summer

S ummer is when the sun comes out,
U p in the sky the sun is shining bright,
M um and Dad are setting the table outside,
M um is lying down getting a tan,
E veryone is running to the ice cream van,
R olling around while playing a water fight.

Stuart Wiseman (9)
Carolside Primary School, Clarkston

Horses

H orses are very friendly animals,
O n the back of a horse is the rider's seat,
R iding through the country,
S ee them galloping along,
E veryone can hear them galloping
                        all night long.

Ananya Kokkranikal (10)
Carolside Primary School, Clarkston

My Friend

A is for Andrew, one of my friends,
N is for neatness made by my friend,
D is for decisions that he always makes,
R is for ready as Andrew always is,
E is for expression, he puts into talks,
W is for waiting, for Andrew is patient,
        All these things are what makes Andrew my friend.

Craig Imrie (10)
Carolside Primary School, Clarkston

My Dog Buddy

My dog Buddy can't control himself,
He rolls in the mud,
But runs about for his own health,
Cos he's my little Bud.

My dog Buddy likes to play ball,
I always throw it down the hall,
He has a monkey which is his best toy,
The monkey's a boy.

After he rolls in the mud,
We'd rather give him a bath,
When he doesn't want one, it's a laugh,
After we clean him, he goes right back into the mud,
But he's still my little Bud.

Stuart Taylor (10)
Carolside Primary School, Clarkston

Tsunami 26/12/04

The tsunami, what a disaster!
Could the waves come any faster?
Just as we feared
As houses disappeared.

The land was bare,
But the waves didn't care,
I shot up a flare,
But no one was there.

On Boxing Day
'Why?' we all pray,
People have died,
We try not to cry.

Calum Husenne (10)
Carolside Primary School, Clarkston

My Best Friend

Aimee is my best friend,
And she will be right to the end,
She comes for sleepovers all the time,
We also make up silly little rhymes.

We're going shopping next weekend,
And she'll come and stay over again,
We'll probably annoy my sister Kate,
And then we'll go to bed late.

I'll talk to Aimee for hours and hours,
As she pretends to have super powers,
My mum gives us a ten minute warning,
As Aimee has to go home in the morning.

Catriona McCallum (10)
Carolside Primary School, Clarkston

Chocolate

C hocolate is sweet like a bag of sweets,
H owever they make it, it is very, very sweet,
O ther people enjoy, other people don't,
C adbury's I recommend is probably the best,
O ver the toffee - melted chocolate drips,
L ots of chocolate is made each and every day,
A ll of them are as sweet as the first,
T o me they are my favourite sweet,
E very little boy and girl likes it.

Jamie Meldrum (10)
Carolside Primary School, Clarkston

Friends

F riends are people who are kind and caring,
R ude people and selfish people are not very fair,
I need to figure out in my mind,
E ither if Stuart and Johnny are actually kind,
N one of my friends are bad,
D on't get a friend who's annoying,
S o watch out who you want to have as a friend.

Euan Waugh (10)
Carolside Primary School, Clarkston

Happiness

A blue sky
Hot spaghetti Bolognese
The smell of perfume
A golden eagle
A new exciting game of hide-and-seek.

Sunita Schrijvers (8)
Conon Bridge Primary School, Dingwall

Sadness . . .

Blue tears stinging my eyes
Cola with no fizz
The smell of chopping onions
Rows of crosses in the graveyard.

Rachel McKay (7)
Conon Bridge Primary School, Dingwall

Anger . . .

As red as a devil from Hell,
Tastes like pickled cabbage for a Saturday meal,
Smells like a stinking, dead duck,
Looks like a burnt-down house,
Sounds like someone dying in war,
Feels like a dragon's foot crushing you.

Jack Cuthbertson (7)
Conon Bridge Primary School, Dingwall

Anger . . .

A red-hot, angry dragon,
Greasy chips and gravy,
A stinking corpse,
Horrible mustard,
A city in ruins.

Christopher Urquhart (7)
Conon Bridge Primary School, Dingwall

Joy . . .

Pink fluffy cushions,
Pizza for dinner every day,
The smell of roses,
Looks like an eagle in the sky,
Birds singing,
Soft feathers on a chick.

Robert McAllister (7)
Conon Bridge Primary School, Dingwall

Anger . . .

Red blood like a snake's bite,
Smells like rotting cucumber,
It tastes like burnt toast,
Like a charging rhinoceros,
Snapping crocodile jaws,
Dragon's breath scorching my skin.

Michael Gillett (7)
Conon Bridge Primary School, Dingwall

Joy . . .

Birds singing in a blue sky,
The tangy taste of bubblegum,
The smell of pizza and chips,
The face on my teacher,
When I give her my maths,
My soft, comfy cushion.

Stephen Greenhowe (7)
Conon Bridge Primary School, Dingwall

Anger . . .

Like the red Devil of Hell,
As sour as lemon juice,
A smell of leftover onions,
A raging bull,
A knife covered in blood,
Shouting and screaming,
Demons getting into my soul.

Kieran McSwegan (7)
Conon Bridge Primary School, Dingwall

Happiness . . .

Blue of the sky,
A fizzy drink at my party,
I like the smell of my mum's perfume,
My cuddly teddy bear,
I like to roll in the snow,
Fairy bells twinkling in the grotto,
Like flying over the moon.

Bethany Skidmore (6)
Conon Bridge Primary School, Dingwall

Anger . . .

A fiery monster spitting flames,
Tastes like a sour sweet,
Smells like rotting beef burgers,
Looks like a black sky with jagged forks of lightning.
Sounds like someone dying,
Feels like an avalanche of rocks.

Andrew Forsyth (7)
Conon Bridge Primary School, Dingwall

Happiness . . .

Yellow sunshine in the summer,
Fresh fish on Fridays,
Fried eggs sizzling,
Playing in the park,
The sound of children laughing,
My soft, comfy chair.

Scott McLaughlin (7)
Conon Bridge Primary School, Dingwall

Swan - Haiku

The swan is swimming,
In the pool of blue water,
A summer's evening.

Lyndsey Gordon **(7)**
Finzean School, Banchory

Springtime Fun - Haiku

Spring is beautiful
In the garden where I play
On a sunny day.

Katie Thow **(7)**
Finzean School, Banchory

Snow - Haiku

The winter snow falls
Down on the ground as we play
On an ice-cold day.

Donna Winton **(7)**
Finzean School, Banchory

Happiness - Haiku

The foal's in the field
Happily playing with Mum,
Beautiful sunshine.

Emma Lawson **(7)**
Finzean School, Banchory

Happy Cow - Haiku

A farm far away
With a happy Highland cow,
Summer sunshine bliss.

Euan Christie (7)
Finzean School, Banchory

Riverbank - Haiku

A flowing river
By the rocky muddy bank
On a rainy day.

Josephine Christie (8)
Finzean School, Banchory

Work Begins - Haiku

Wet snow melting fast
Tractor starting to work hard
In the springtime breeze.

Alistair Winton (8)
Finzean School, Banchory

Jets Flying Fast - Haiku

Jets flying so fast
At Scotland's RAF base
On March the thirteenth.

Neil Thomson-Mitchell (8)
Finzean School, Banchory

Waves - Haiku

Waves crash hard and loud
At the end of the grey rocks;
A stormy, cold day.

Marianne Mackie (8)
Finzean School, Banchory

Rabbit - Haiku

A bouncing rabbit
In its brightly coloured hutch
On a winter's day.

Jodie Maher (8)
Finzean School, Banchory

Trees - Haiku

Trees sway by the breeze
Singing a beautiful song
On the hills today.

Erin Lloyd (8)
Finzean School, Banchory

The Seasons

Spring is here and lambs born,
Summer is here and sunflowers are growing,
Autumn is here and leaves are falling,
Winter is here and a new year begins.

Emma Baillie (7)
Head of Muir Primary School, Denny

The Seasons

In spring Easter comes and flowers grow again
and lambs are born.
In summer butterflies flutter by and roses grow.
In autumn leaves change colour and swirl down
to the ground and Hallowe'en spooks frighten us.
In winter Santa delivers presents and Jesus was born.

Dayna Leckie (7)
Head of Muir Primary School, Denny

The Seasons

In spring lambs are born
and Easter is a time for fun.
In summer sunflowers grow tall
over the wall and daisies grow as well.
In autumn on Bonfire Night the sky is bright
and the fireworks go to a high height.
In winter snowmen are built across the snow covered grass.

Alasdair Pemble (7)
Head of Muir Primary School, Denny

The Seasons

In spring Easter eggs are cracked and flowers
Pop out of the ground.
In summer the sun is shining on us.
We put suncream on,
In autumn leaves flutter down
And Hallowe'en spooks . . . scream!
In winter we throw snowballs and build snowmen.

Ross Weir (7)
Head of Muir Primary School, Denny

The Seasons

Spring is here and baby lambs are born,
Summer is here and sunflowers grow tall,
Autumn is here and leaves change colour,
Winter is here and Santa comes.

Daniel MacFarlane (7)
Head of Muir Primary School, Denny

The Seasons

Spring is here and the birds are building their nests,
Summer is here and the butterflies say hello,
Autumn is here and the leaves flutter by,
Winter is here and in the snow we go sledging.

Sophie Rawding (7)
Head of Muir Primary School, Denny

The Seasons

In spring Easter comes and birds build their nests,
In summer we have our holidays and butterflies flutter by,
In autumn golden leaves swirl off the trees and it's Bonfire Night,
In winter Santa delivers presents to happy children and
We build snowmen.

Chloe White (6)
Head of Muir Primary School, Denny

The Seasons

Spring is here and Easter is coming,
Summer is here and bees go buzzing,
Autumn is here and apples are growing,
Winter is here and snow is falling.

John Campbell (7)
Head of Muir Primary School, Denny

The Seasons

Spring is here and the birds build their nests,
Summer is here and we play in the sun,
Autumn is here and the leaves fall off the trees,
Winter is here and we ski on the hill.

Iain Crossan (7)
Head of Muir Primary School, Denny

The Seasons

In spring flowers grow and Easter is here,
In summer sunflowers grow and bees fly by,
In autumn leaves fall down on the ground
And Hallowe'en spooks us,
In winter snowflakes fall and we make snowmen.

David Cunningham (7)
Head of Muir Primary School, Denny

The Seasons

In spring the lambs are born and Easter comes,
Summer is here and bees buzz by,
Autumn is here and leaves fall off the trees as they change colour,
Winter is here and the snowflakes flutter to the ground.

Ruth Dyson (7)
Head of Muir Primary School, Denny

The Seasons

Spring is here and bluebells grow in the woods,
Summer is here and sunflowers grow up high with the sun shining,
Autumn is here and the leaves change colour,
Winter is here and snow comes down from the sky.

Eilidh Ferguson (7)
Head of Muir Primary School, Denny

The Seasons

In spring lambs are born and it's Easter,
In summer we have our holidays and bees fly by,
In autumn the leaves change and Hallowe'en spooks us,
In winter the trees grow bare and we make snowmen.

Blair Forbes **(7)**
Head of Muir Primary School, Denny

The Seasons

Spring flowers, lambs are born,
Summer is hot, lots of people go on holiday,
Autumn leaves change colour,
Winter, Santa comes and gives us presents.

Ross Gray **(7)**
Head of Muir Primary School, Denny

The Seasons

In spring Easter comes and baby lambs are born,
In summer we go on holidays and butterflies flutter by,
In autumn leaves change colour like red, gold and brown,
In winter we run down the stairs having so much fun.

Kirsten Harrower **(7)**
Head of Muir Primary School, Denny

The Seasons

In spring Easter comes and the lambs are born,
In summer we have our holidays and butterflies flutter by,
In autumn the leaves fall on the ground,
In winter we put up decorations.

Kiranjeet Kaur **(7)**
Head of Muir Primary School, Denny

I Am Happy!

I feel happy, I feel sad,
I got a new football,
And now I am football mad!
If you want to play,
Then come this way,
And if you burst my ball,
Then you will have to pay,
I am going to the park,
Which isn't very far,
If you want to come,
Well then come on then,
Oh, I love football!

Connor Mitchell (11)
Head of Muir Primary School, Denny

I Feel Scared

I feel frightened,
I feel worried,
I feel scared,
Not a word, not a soul knows,
How I feel right here, right now . . .

Sometimes I feel sad,
Sometimes I feel left out,
I just feel scared.

Jill Hunter (11)
Head of Muir Primary School, Denny

Father Apart

You were there when I was born,
You were the one who brought me up,
You were the one who gave me a home,
A life as well.
You took me on holidays,
You took me far,
And most of all you gave me your love,
But why did it have to end like this?

Scott Shanks (10)
Head of Muir Primary School, Denny

Boring School

School!
Need to do work,
So boring!
Then some rest from work,
At playtime.
But back onto work again,
At last home time, that is the best!
Go home and get out of school clothes,
Next day back to school, boring!

Alana Galbraith (10)
Head of Muir Primary School, Denny

Filled With Happiness

Yippee, yahoo,
This is the happiest day of my life,
I'm getting a puppy,
Yippee, yahoo.
Today it is,
Today it is.
My legs are crossed,
My legs are crossed.
I am so excited too,
At the same time I am nervous,
I mean, really nervous,
Here I go, here I go.
Now I've got my puppy!
I am going to play and play with him all day,
I'll feed him and brush him and groom him,
Until he's all nice and fresh,
Now that he is home, I am so happy,
He will be in my life all the time.

Eve Whitelaw (11)
Head of Muir Primary School, Denny

The Seasons

In spring baby lambs are born and
blossom grows on the trees,
In summer lots of people go on holiday
and butterflies flutter by,
In autumn leaves fall off the trees and
they change colours like gold, brown and red,
In winter sometimes it snows and a new year begins.

Jenna Douglas (7)
Head of Muir Primary School, Denny

Year After Year

Year after year children
Collect from me
My shiny, two-toned conkers.

Year after year children
Sit under me
On my long, hard roots,
That go miles into the ground.

Year after year
In my own special way
I wave to children
As they walk past me.

Year after year
In the crisp snow
Children build snowmen
Next to me,
And then I just
Watch them fade away
And wait for another year.

Teddi Anderson (10)
Kincardine-in-Menteith Primary School, Stirling

Sycamore Tree

The tree leans,
It is old and dry,
Knobbly, thin branches,
Become big and old.

Its leaves are soft,
Really dry,
They are cold,
Like freezing metal,
The leaves are so big,
They could probably fly!

Sean McBeath (8)
Kincardine-in-Menteith Primary School, Stirling

The Millennium Tree

So petite it is
But wonderful
A spectacular sight
Just standing there
A memorial to the
Millennium.

Just a young child
Only four years old
But with its
Precious leaves.

The roots
Under the ground
Tangling with other roots
Pushing and pulling
To find the best path
Like a bird finding its nest.

The surroundings are beautiful,
Greens, browns, golden,
Just a perfect collage
But the tree is still
One of a kind.

James McBeath (11)
Kincardine-in-Menteith Primary School, Stirling

My Special Tree

There it is as high as three ladders on top of each other
The leaves like a polished brass doorknob
The trunk as small as a step with ridges and bumps in it
Leaves like a fan swaying in the wind
I feel happy when I climb it,but it is very tall.

Phil Aitken (9)
Kincardine-in-Menteith Primary School, Stirling

Oak Tree

My acorns fall from me,
Bursting all the way through their shells,
Rolling around the roads and lanes,
Cars running over my precious treasures.

They try to run away,
There is no wind to blow them away,
They're shouting, 'Help! Help!'
Nobody hears them shouting for help.

Then the wind comes back,
That doesn't make me worry so much,
I'm sure they have made it,
I wish I could save them.

The ones that are there
I hope they are safe,
People collecting them,
I have one baby left.

My leaves have disappeared,
One by one they fall to the ground
Hiding my treasures,
They have all gone and disappeared.

Amanda Killen (10)
Kincardine-in-Menteith Primary School, Stirling

The Tree

This brilliant tree used to be a seed,
Not like a stupid, stupid weed,
It grew very tall,
Even bigger than a mall.

It liked to dance with his friend the sun,
Before he was turned into a kitchen table.
He had a shiny apple hanging from his branch,
So he bit it and went *crunch, crunch, crunch.*

The tree said to the sun,
'I don't want to be a kitchen table!'
Then the evil men came
And destroyed all day.
When they left the tree opened his eyes
And said, 'I'm not dead!'

So the next day the tree said to the sun,
'I've got this shooting pain in my legs!
Please help me sun, those evil men are killing me!'
The next day the sun woke up
And said, 'Tree, where have you gone?'
There was no answer.

Struan Scott (11)
Kippen Primary School, Stirling

Murder

The beauty of a tree is infinite,
But the heart of a greedy human is not.
The trees hold homes and food,
The humans hold axes and money.

The trees are stuck and being hunted down,
The human striking blows.
The humans smile as money flows in,
But as the trees cry their last,
They call money a sin.

The humans move away from the barren landscape
And think they have done their job.
The place is bare but not for long,
For saplings emerge from the ground,
They sing and dance for joy,
For the evil ones have gone.

But their ancestors still are lost,
They cry and wail for they know now
The rainforest is also lost.

Maura Collins (11)
Kippen Primary School, Stirling

The Talking Tree

As high as you could ever see,
Is the size of the talking tree,
It goes to the locals and eats all the stock,
Will that tree ever stop?

It jumps and talks and plays all day,
Everyone wishes it would go away,
It sings at night and no one can sleep,
When it's told to stop singing it starts to weep.

The lumberjack came to the forest that day,
Everyone says take the talking tree away,
The talking tree ran as fast as it could,
The lumberjack said, 'No,' but everyone insisted he should.

The talking tree had eventually stopped,
It couldn't support itself so it dropped,
The village people heard a crash,
They ran to the noise in a dash.

There they saw the talking tree,
Looking up it couldn't believe what it could see,
There it was,a spiky saw,
No one even said, 'Aww.'
That was the end of the talking tree,
It was made into furniture,
For you and me.

Robert Kilpatrick (11)
Kippen Primary School, Stirling

The Evil Fig Tree

The strangular fig
Grows down other trees
Until it reaches the ground
But after that it
Grows back up
And kills the things that
Gave it life,
It grows big and strong
And hollow
Until it gets cut down
And now we see
The murderer being
Murdered.
It wails and screams
And cries
And thunders to
The ground,
And as it wails and wails,
The people don't care.

Daniel McBride (11)
Kippen Primary School, Stirling

The Tree

This tree is alive
There is no doubt
But soon its life will be taken,
Taken right out.

It can hear the sound of a chainsaw
Cutting down its neighbours,
Taking away their lives, their homes,
Their shelter.

The animals that live on this tree start to leave,
They tell the tree they're sorry
But they can't risk their lives
For it.

It wails, it cries, it howls,
It doesn't want to be cut down.
The noise of the rainforest drowns out its yells,
No one knows its life is at an end.

Beth Finlay (11)
Kippen Primary School, Stirling

Tree Sounds

Crunch, the sound of the birds
As they munch the berries from the tall, strong tree.
Famished, overnight they gorge at the treetop.
Flap, flap as the birds fly away at the slightest sounds.
The tree, shivering at the prospect of cutters,
Rumbling, the sound of cutters coming.
Chop! The sound of life coming out of the tree,
Like blood from a man.

Jack Turner (11)
Kippen Primary School, Stirling

Culmailie

I see the water slowly swaying down the burn,
The rain smashing off the sea making ripples as far as I can see,
I see the mountain tall and shadowing in the sunlight,
The house, small and isolated between the two mountains.

The stew with vegetables newly picked from the fields,
I taste the smoked bacon, tasty and fresh,
The fish recently smoked from the smoke house,
I taste the water from the sea, salty and dirty,
It makes my thirst run for the hills.

I feel the soft, silky sand as it clings to my feet as they are still,
The dirt up from the sea, wet, musky, golden brown,
I run back into the cold shimmering sea to wash myself of the mud,
I clamber over the rock hurting my feet on the rough
Surface but still avoid the sand.

I hear the trees noisily swaying side to side,
The wind howling round the mountains,
I hear the boat bouncing on every wave that hits it,
The piglets howling in the wind.

I smell the air - fresh, still and gentle,
The wool freshly clipped from the sheep,
I smell the fish recently caught and luscious for my lips,
The smoke from the chimney fills my lungs with soot.

Ethan Carle (11)
Kirklandpark Primary School, Strathaven

Culmailie

I see the gigantic frozen mountains in their proud scenery,
The tired dirty animals lazing about.
The wavy sea is calmly relaxed as it is feeding the fish,
The old, still trees look grumpy and miserable as they sway in the wind.

I taste the rich, tender stew melt in my mouth, as I chew
The unpleasant breeze of salt fills my mouth
And is still as strong as ever,
The warm porridge bursts into my taste buds as I enjoy every spoonful,
I can still taste that heavenly bite of the fresh, salty fish.

I feel the hard rugged boat roughly scrape against my hands,
As it sways through the water,
The sand falling through my hands like the cold winter's rain,
The green leaves lie on my hands as they fall asleep,
The tickly, comfy grass comforts me as I feel the life within it.

I hear the wind whistle into my ears, moaning and blowing,
I hear the cows sneezing and snorting as they try to fall asleep
in the field,
The stream trickling and gurgling as the water tries to dodge
the stones,
The fire spitting and snapping as it burns the wood.

I smell the pleasant scent of the multicoloured flowers travel
up my nose,
The smelly, damp, musty smell still lurks around me,
The sweet vegetable smell as good as it's always been,
That roasted salt-mutton is a bite of Heaven.

Gregor Stirling (10)
Kirklandpark Primary School, Strathaven

Culmailie

I see the shining sun floating in the sky,
The puffy clouds bobbing up and down,
The light, clear blocks of rain,
The lumpy, round and rough hills.

I taste the salty, sandy, dirty sea,
The bumpy, milky, sugary porridge,
The clear, fresh, still water,
The smoky, meaty, thick bacon.

I touch the fluffy, cloudy, tangled wool as soft as feathers,
I feel the long, hairy, spiky grass,
The uncomfortable, jaggy, raggy covers,
The soft, wet, cotton-like animals.

I smell lumps, heaps, piles of coal
And wet, stinky, honky pigs,
The sooty, black coal fire smoking,
The wet, smelly, mucky dogs jumping up and licking you.

I hear feet stamping and mooing, grumpy cows
And roaring, whistling, blowing wind,
The splashing, slashing, soaring sea,
The blowing, roaring, grumbling trees.

Daniel Harris (10)
Kirklandpark Primary School, Strathaven

Don't Blame It On Me

Last week's plate has gone all mouldy,
Tiptoeing into the kitchen for some grub,
Seven squashed peas on the floor,
'Don't blame it on me!'

A pile of clothes like a mountain on the bed,
A maze of CDs on the floor,
Reading, maths and much more piled upon my desk,
'Don't blame it on me!'

Broke the picture on the wall,
Oh no, baby's gone up the stair,
She could have fell from there,
'Don't blame it on me!'

Toothpaste has gone all dry,
Shampoo spilled on the floor,
Mum's good perfume sprayed on the door,
'Don't blame it on me!'

Martha Smart (11)
Kirklandpark Primary School, Strathaven

Culmailie

I hear the fire blazing, roaring, sparkling as it has just been lit,
The wind whistling, howling, singing a tune,
Hens clucking and pecking their food,
The waves lapping on the shore and slapping against the rocks.

I taste the fresh, cold water from the burn,
Warm, salty porridge melting in my mouth,
Smoky and fatty pig freshly cooked by Mum,
The salty water splashing gently on me from the sea.

I see the big, red sunset sinking away,
Tall, steep mountains with a glistening cover of snow,
Seagulls swooping noisily down to the water,
The tree branches moving wildly and fiercely whacking against
the wind.

I touch the gritty, dry sand pouring out of my hand,
Smooth, oval pebbles scattered on the beach,
Rough branches scratching my arm as they blow in the wind,
The cold, trickling water running through the burn.

Jessica Duff (10)
Kirklandpark Primary School, Strathaven

I Wouldn't Do That!

Sneaking food from the cupboard,
Thick, sticky sauce on the table,
Things in huge heaps on the counter,
'I wouldn't do that!'

Dirty washing piled like sandbags in a flood,
PlayStation games lying everywhere,
Shoes scattered everywhere just like seeds,
'I wouldn't do that!'

Toothpaste on the mirror like thick snow in winter,
Bubble bath making the floor slippy,
Bath overflowing like Angel Falls,
'I wouldn't do that!'

Mucky fingerprints on the table,
Pen on the sofa like great railway tracks,
Hidden remotes in all sorts of places,
'I wouldn't do that!'

Euan Paterson (11)
Kirklandpark Primary School, Strathaven

It Was James!

Yogurt all over, slowly making its way down the walls like slugs,
Smoke everywhere because chocolate's been in the
Microwave too long,
Bottle of wine smashed all over the floor - very messy!
'It was James!'

Potion made of cream, juice, tissues and food in a big bowl!
Clothes slung on the sofa in one, big, messy heap,
Jug of water spilled on the floor making a big puddle,
'It was James!'

Letting the cat in the good room to rip the wrapping paper
Off the presents,
Fiddling with the lights,
Sitting on the arm rest on the new sofas,
'It was James!'

Using Mum's favourite bubble bath - all gone in the time of a second,
Swapping over all the sprays,
Taking nail clippers and losing them,
'It was James!'

Ellie Lee (11)
Kirklandpark Primary School, Strathaven

Culmailie

I touch the clean, cold water that has been taken from the fresh burn,
I run my fingers through the horse's soft, shiny mane,
I pick up some thin, sparkly sand,
It finely runs through my fingers back onto the beach,
I take a hard, shiny rock from the ground and throw it against
The hard, wooden wall of the animal pen.

I hear the wind moaning and whispering,
Almost as if it is trying to tell me a secret,
The cow lowing and stomping her feet, as she wants some food,
I hear the water bubbling and flowing nicely,
It's splashing off the rocks, giving me a spray of water,
The trees are banging together and their crisp orange
And yellow autumn leaves are rustling.

I see the massive green mountains with a bit of white snow
Lying on top of them,
People working away and making a great job,
I see a glimmering big sun which is setting in-between
The two, enormous mountains.

I taste the salt of the sea in my mouth,
The smoky, crisp bacon ready to eat,
The big, warm pot of salty porridge Mum made me earlier,
I taste the rough, salty fish which was just caught this morning,
Still slippery, about to fall off my plate!

I smell the wild flowers in the luscious green fields that smell so fresh,
The smell of my mum's mouth-watering cooking,
I feel hungry now . . .
I smell the horrible stench of the pig coming from the barn,
The smoky, sooty fire burning and crackling.

Georgia McKay (11)
Kirklandpark Primary School, Strathaven

Culmailie

I hear the sea smashing against the rocks, roaring in and out,
The wind howling, whistling, playing its own little tune,
The fire crackling inside the house, spitting and hissing,
The pig snorting, stamping and squealing for food.

I see the house, old, dark and all alone,
The boat swaying in the water, lonely and empty,
The hills still and silent, towering above me,
The sea rough as ever, rushing back and forth.

I touch the dry, gritty sand so fine as it just falls through my fingers,
The rocks, hard, bumpy and uneven giving me grazes as I touch them,
The animal's coats wet from the rain, all matted and unfine,
The wood from the shed, smooth and textured
As I run my hand along it.

I smell the briny seaweed, salty from the sea,
The peat on the fire, smoky and horrible,
The air fresh, clean and crisp as it blows in my face,
The house musty and peaty from the fire.

I taste the warm, fresh stew bubbling above the fire,
The water, fresh and clean from the trickling burn,
The bacon, smoky and tough to chew,
The fish, fresh and salty straight from the sea.

Karen Adamson (11)
Kirklandpark Primary School, Strathaven

Culmailie

I can see the sea slapping against the rocks
And the sun up above shining in the shimmering sky,
The trees swaying back and forth,
The horse trotting, galloping away from the seashore into the distance.

I can taste the smoked bacon from the pigs,
The sheep's mutton, salty and rough,
Splashes from the firth in my mouth,
It tastes salty, bitter, but fresh.

I can touch the smooth, yellow, soft sand between my fingers,
The rough feathers from the hens,
I can feel the coarse coat of the cow as well.

I can hear the wind whistling through the branches of the bare trees,
The animals outside groaning, squealing for food,
I can also hear the fire crackling, sizzling, sparkling in my room.

I can smell the animal's food from outside, it smells fresh and sweet,
The salty, seaweedy smell from the sea,
The sweet, refreshing fragrance of the flowers coming through
                                                    our house,
The fishy, salty smell from the fish that my dad had caught for
                                                    our dinner.

Amy Sterritt (11)
Kirklandpark Primary School, Strathaven

Er, Oops!

Food flying out of shelves and into my mouth,
Peas on my spoon and I'm taking aim,
Cooker firing up like a volcano, doesn't bother me,
'Er, oops!'

It's a rainforest of clothes and books,
The desk is messy with piled up pens,
There's a whole different world underneath the couch,
'Er, oops!'

Toilet roll lying on the floor like a snake,
Taps left running and it's draining the Pacific,
Towels scattered all across the floor,
'Er, oops!'

The sofa is covered with jam and juice stains,
The TV's got fingermarks from left to right,
The remote controls are left all around the house,
'Er, oops!'

Alistair Coull (11)
Kirklandpark Primary School, Strathaven

Kittens

They play and run about the room,
When they're around there's no gloom,
I have to pick one, oh, but whom?

Soon he'll grow into a cat
And stretch out over the mat,
He'll run and jump and never get fat.

He'll eat any sort of cat food,
He'd never get in a mood
And they are definitely not rude!

Melanie Murray (10)
Leith Walk Primary School, Edinburgh

Jawbreaker

Jawbreaker, Jawbreaker,
Nice to eat.

Jawbreaker, Jawbreaker,
I never greet.

Jawbreaker, Jawbreaker,
Fat, full of candy.

Jawbreaker, Jawbreaker,
Great and grandy!

Jawbreaker, Jawbreaker,
I love it.

Jawbreaker, Jawbreaker,
I bite it.

Jawbreaker, Jawbreaker,
Makes me fat.

Jawbreaker, Jawbreaker,
Don't be like that!

Jawbreaker, Jawbreaker,
Hard and round.

Jawbreaker, Jawbreaker,
I'm glad you're found.

Tammy Walker (10)
Leith Walk Primary School, Edinburgh

Family

Family, family loving and caring,
Family, family sometimes daring,
Family, family four in a bunch,
Family, family I'd eat them for lunch!

Mum, Mum she ain't dumb, .
Mum, Mum she's so fun,
Mum, Mum sometimes a pain,
Mum, Mum she's not lame.

Family, family loving and caring,
Family, family sometimes daring,
Family, family four in a bunch,
Family, family I'd eat them for lunch!

Dad, Dad he's so mad,
Dad, Dad but I'm glad,
Dad, Dad he's gone bonkers,
Dad, Dad he's lost his conkers.

Family, family loving and caring,
Family, family sometimes daring,
Family, family four in a bunch,
Family, family I'd eat them for lunch!

Sadie, Sadie she acts like a lady,
Sadie, Sadie she's a big baby,
Sadie, Sadie she is weird,
Sadie, Sadie she's growing a beard!

Family, family loving and caring,
Family, family sometimes daring,
Family, family four in a bunch,
Family, family I'd eat them for lunch!

Jack Shearer (10)
Leith Walk Primary School, Edinburgh

Best Friend

Best friend, best friend, faithful and trusted,
Best friend, best friend, never get busted,
Best friend, best friend, helpful and kind,
Best friend, best friend, always binds.

Harpreet, Harpreet loves to eat noodles,
Harpreet, Harpreet admires a dog called Doodles,
Harpreet, Harpreet loves shopping,
Harpreet, Harpreet also likes hopping.

Best friend, best friend, faithful and trusted,
Best friend, best friend, never gets busted,
Best friend, best friend, helpful and kind,
Best friend, best friend, always binds.

Melanie, Melanie loves gold,
Melanie, Melanie is easily cold,
Melanie, Melanie is so wild,
Melanie, Melanie could be mild.

Lipa Hussain (10)
Leith Walk Primary School, Edinburgh

Fear

Fear is dark blue
Like a cold sky.

Fear smells like
Rusting metal.

Fear feels like a cold blade
Being pushed through you.

Fear tastes like sand
From a dry desert.

Murray Willis (11)
Lismore Primary School, Argyll

Steam Trains

Listening for the steam train's hissing brakes
As it pulls up at the station platform,
When it sets off it rattles and shakes,
I feel really warm with fun and laughter,
The smoke stays behind a long time after,
Along comes the ticket man clipping all the tickets,
I trust the steam train strong and fast,
How long until we get there?
I hope the journey will last!

Joe Derham (11)
Lismore Primary School, Argyll

Sadness

Sadness feels like you are nothing,
It sounds like lots of voices talking,
But none of them to you,
It tastes like vinegar, sour on your tongue,
Sadness feels like you are nothing.

Eilidh Willis (9)
Lismore Primary School, Argyll

Trapped!

The wind blew the sea into angry waves,
Houses shook, windows creaked.
The tree so tall fell on my road home,
I was trapped!
Two strong men with torches came for me,
Clambering through the branches,
Now I'm safe at home.

John Carmichael (9)
Lismore Primary School, Argyll

Anger

Anger feels rough and dim,
It makes your eyes fire-red,
It smells spicy and hot,
I cannot control anger.

It's like I'm living in a dark place
And I'm stuck forever in this small room.
When I get angry
The sky goes black and everything burns,
I cannot control anger.

It smells like burning smoke
And it makes me want to breathe out fire,
I must control my anger,
The world must control its anger.

Calum McGillivray (10)
Lismore Primary School, Argyll

Sadness

Sadness is a light shade of blue,
Sadness is like the last leaf of the old oak tree
Falling to the ground,
Sadness sounds like a repetitive beating in my ear
That I can't escape,
Sadness reminds me of the sun setting
And not coming back,
Sadness feels like the cold, salty spray of the sea
Landing gently on my face.
Sadness is a feeling that is very powerful
And can only be used with great emotion.

Keiran McLarney (11)
Lismore Primary School, Argyll

Space

Space is cold and black
Like a massive, dark bottomless pit,
It is so huge it feels like the ocean on a midsummer evening.
The sun and the Earth are so different;
Earth, a marble, spinning through time and space.
The sun is like a glowing lamp, lighting up space around it.
I feel like I am weightless, floating in space.

I feel so tiny and insignificant, space is all around me,
I feel like I'll be sucked up, with all the planets next to me
I feel that space is incredible, stretching out beside me.
Space is great,
Tremendous and dominant.

Emma Sanderson (9)
Lismore Primary School, Argyll

Wild Weather

In
the springtime
leaves open
all over the floor
making a horrible mess.
Luckily we have
a cleaner.

Gales
are blowing.
It's nearly spring
no wonder it is so
cold, so cold it
might snow, I
hope it
will!

Alannah Warner (9)
Marybank Primary School, Muir of Ord

Winter

W inter is very windy,
  I t is more windy than expected.
N aked
T rees shifting side to side.
E nergy
R unning through the air.

Jessica Dean (9)
Marybank Primary School, Muir of Ord

Winter

A snowman is made
With big balls of snow
Coming down from the sky.

The snow is something fun and special.
Snow isn't something you can just throw away.
Snow is great.

Andrew Brown (9)
Marybank Primary School, Muir of Ord

Winter Wonderland

W inter is wonderful and lots of fun.
  I ce covers the small garden pond.
N ew snow covers the valley.
T rees stand bare, no leaves in sight.
E ver falling snow hits the ground
R esting on the subtle earth.

Zoe Thorpe (9)
Marybank Primary School, Muir of Ord

Wild Winter

Snow is falling, winter comes,
Missing apples, missing plums,
Sleeping bears, wolves and more,
Missing cubs, cold and sore.

Children playing in the snow,
People coming to say hello,
Hanging down icicles large or small,
Some on my house, some in the hall!

Grandad sleeping in his armchair,
Grandma's cooking but Grandad doesn't care,
Frozen water, frozen fish,
Now it's time to make my wish.

Emily Brydon (9)
Marybank Primary School, Muir of Ord

Winter

Winter is coming, snow is falling,
The ground is turning white.
Snow is white and very bright,
It lightens up the sky.
When we all go out to play
The snow is very deep.
When you make a snowman,
Don't forget his nose
And don't let the dogs tickle his toes!

Louise Muirhead (8)
Marybank Primary School, Muir of Ord

Wonderful Winter

W inter is wonderful and fun!
 I ce covers the park pond!
N ow snowmen stand in the garden!
 T rees are bare and there isn't a leaf in sight!
 E lves are down in their underground towns!
 R unners are tucked up in front of the fire!

Marsaili Stewart-Skinner (9)
Marybank Primary School, Muir of Ord

Early In The Morning

My mother made my breakfast,
Early in the morning.
I wait nervously for the train,
Early in the morning.
I took a whiff of dear old London,
Early in the morning.
I'm going on the black steam train,
Early in the morning.
I'm sitting on the soft, red seat,
Early in the morning.
I'm listening to the loud gunshots,
Early in the morning.
I pass some worried faces and some gloomy slums,
Early in the morning.
I arrive at my new airy house,
Late in the evening.

Lynn Smith (9)
Meadowburn Primary School, Bishopbriggs

A Big Surprise!

Terrible tasteless toffee is all I have to eat,
Oh what would I give now for a bowl of mother's milk and wheat.
My ancient tweed trousers are starting to itch,
All this marching around is giving me a stitch.

Outside there's rain, lightning and thunder,
What will my new life be like, I wonder?
There are the women, choosing the kids,
Like chattering seagulls they're placing their bids.

The smell of the sweat is extremely strong,
Although the farmers' wives' perfume makes a bit of a pong!
The village hall is packed like sardines in a can,
My best friend, Alfie, has been driven away in a van.

There goes funny little Jenny and the raving monster Gwen,
The number of us tramping round has narrowed down to ten.
Off go the curly-haired Harrison twins
And three little girls clutching their money tins.

Four little boys and one little girlie,
A man chooses her because her hair is long and curly.
Only four of us left plodding round,
I'd never do this again, even for a pound!

A young girl comes and takes the Johnstone brothers three,
Only one person left; that person is me.
The hall is empty, there's no one there now,
Mr MacNeil says, 'Why did this happen? And how?'

When I ask him what's wrong, he says with a grin,
'Anyone who's left behind, I said I'd take in!'

Eilidh Munro (11)
Meadowburn Primary School, Bishopbriggs

Who Will It Be?

I can see a lot of people smiling sweetly,
But who will it be?
Will it be that old man with a long beard
Or could it be that big lady wearing my mum's favourite green hat?
I think I know whom it will be to take me home,
It will be that young lady I can hear talking to me.

Where will we go?
I feel very nervous but excited at the same time,
Will we go to a big house
With butlers, maids and cooks?
Or will it be a cottage
Beside the whooshing sea?
I can feel my brother's cold hand
Getting warmer inside mine
As we get closer to the car.

It is like
My own warm, cosy home
With the blazing fire,
The lovely smell of home baking
And fresh cut grass.
I eat my mince and tatties
And think of my mother and father,
I miss them,
I desperately want to go home.

Heather Kindness (10)
Meadowburn Primary School, Bishopbriggs

Evacuee

I am feeling quite distressed as
I leave the city behind.
As the train chugs along
The buildings shrink in size.

I can smell the burning coal
And it's choking me.
It reminds me of the fire that
I used to have at home.

I'm keeping a firm grip
On my heavy case.
My brown gas mask box
Is hanging from my neck.

Jamie Murray (10)
Meadowburn Primary School, Bishopbriggs

Leaving Home

I'm leaving my home
With a small case in my hand.
There's a brown box
Round my neck with a gas mask inside.

There is a lot of sandwiches
On the big, long train.
Mine are jam and butter,
My brother has the same.

I am walking in a circle,
I don't know if I'll be chosen.
I am feeling tearful,
I miss my mum and dad.

James Morrison (9)
Meadowburn Primary School, Bishopbriggs

Evacuation

My case is very heavy,
My gas mask's in its box,
The brown box hanging around my neck
Is giving me a bruise.

I'm sitting at the train track.
Holding my mother's hand,
I see a lot of children
Playing gleefully.

I'm sitting on the train
Eating a cheese sandwich,
I hear a loud *choo, choo.*
I wave goodbye to Mum.

The train is slowing down now,
I look outside the window,
I see some lovely flowers,
I'm sure my mum will love them.

Fraser Munro (9)
Meadowburn Primary School, Bishopbriggs

Leaving My Life

I'm standing by the railway,
My mother's by my side,
The big, tall steam train is
Rushing down the wooden track.

I'm sitting on the comfy seat
And we are all squashed together,
Children sobbing loudly,
Waving goodbyes to mothers.

The full train's preparing to leave,
I smell the coal burning at the front
Like the warm fire in my home.

Smoke billows from the top
And comes through the window
Down into my mouth,
I taste the soggy sandwiches
My mother packed for me.

Ishbal MacLennan (10)
Meadowburn Primary School, Bishopbriggs

A New Life

The train pulled to a halt,
The smell of sweat and salt.
My stomach's in pain as I get off the train,
I sit on a seat and start to eat.
I go to the hall where we are all
Told to walk and not talk.
A family come and look,
They say, 'OK, let's go and book.'
On the way home we pass the lake,
My host mother puts a pie on to bake.
The cottage is very pretty,
It's got a thatched roof.
I can hear the church bells
Ringing in the distance.
I feel very lonely,
I wish I was back home.

Hannah Macintosh (9)
Meadowburn Primary School, Bishopbriggs

Like I Am Stuck In A Box

In the darkest,
Loneliest
Part of the class corner
Sits a very lonely boy,
Nobody likes him or cares for him,
Not even the teacher,
He does not even like himself,
He thinks he's a worthless piece of dirt.

Bruce Gibson (10)
Muirtown Primary School, Inverness

The Lonely Child

Sitting on the bench in the playground
Watching the world go by,
All the time I do this, wondering why.
I don't have any friends
Because they think I'm different,
The children go past me,
They make me upset when they say horrible things.
They don't know I'm the same as them,
I hope this day ends.

I'm better off without these bullies anyway.

Ethan Turner (9)
Muirtown Primary School, Inverness

Standing In The Playground

Standing in the playground
Watching people play,
Watching them for hours
Every single day.
Wishing I could play,
When the bell rings
I walk slowly, quietly
And sadly to the class.
When it's time to go home
I am still very sad.

Aiden Lyall (9)
Muirtown Primary School, Inverness

Sad And Lonely

Sitting at a table,
Sitting on my own,
Watching the people I know,
Laughing . . .
I don't.
Chatting . . .
I don't.
I'll sit here till the bell rings.
Now I am making my way up to class,
Dreading what is planned for me,
Is anyone else
Sad?
Lonely?
Does anyone care?

Caitlin MacColl (9)
Muirtown Primary School, Inverness

I Am Really Sad

All on my own
in the playground,
with nobody to play
with or talk to.
And now the bell
has gone and everyone
is running to the lines.
I walk into the classroom,
slowly and sadly
and take my coat and shoes off.

Hazel Blackhall (9)
Muirtown Primary School, Inverness

The Same Old Day

Every day at 9 o'clock
In the school
In the middle of the playground
Watching the balls go past
Watching people play
With their friends
Nothing to do all day
Just the same old day.

Graeme Goddard (9)
Muirtown Primary School, Inverness

All Alone

No one here, I am just all alone
Waiting for a friend to appear.
The bell just went, everyone lines up
And I still feel all alone.
I walk to the classroom slowly, sadly
And I think not one bit of my life has changed.

Ellie Munro (9)
Muirtown Primary School, Inverness

I Am Sad

Standing in the rain
Watching people play,
Nobody to talk to
And nobody to play with,
Waiting until the bell goes.
When the bell goes
People push me to the end of the line.

Amy Anderson (9)
Muirtown Primary School, Inverness

Best Friends

When you are sad or lonely
There is always someone.
There's your mum to your
Best friend.

You go and play and make
Best friend necklaces and
Models of you and your
Best friend.

You say to your best friend
You are never alone, you have
God beside you and me.

Just be kind and you will fit
In just fine, that is you and
       Me.

Erin Wardlaw (9)
Muirtown Primary School, Inverness

Lonely Child

Standing in the playground
Watching people play.
No friends, no nothing,
Not even a speck of rain.
There goes the bell,
I need to get inside.
I walk in the classroom,
I sit down at my desk,
The teacher says,
'Get your work done.'

Anna Bown (9)
Muirtown Primary School, Inverness

Only Me

I am in the playground
All on my own,
Standing watching
Everyone else.
I sat on the grass
But no one would
Look at me.
I heard the bell
So I changed
My shoes
And went
Up to class
Slowly, sadly
And quietly.

Bobby Chisholm (9)
Muirtown Primary School, Inverness

Lonely In School

I open my eyes and get out of bed,
Dress myself and then get fed.
I leave the house and walk to school
With no friends beside me I feel like a fool.

I get into school and go to my class
Thinking what could I ask.
I am still thinking about my maths
What will I do? Don't have clue!

Kieran Macgillivray (9)
Muirtown Primary School, Inverness

Standing In The Playground

Standing in the playground
Watching people play,
Watching them for hours
Every single day.
Walking into the classroom
With my head bowed.
Watching all my classmates
Talking to each other
And just as usual
I'm left in the corner.
I just wish I had a friend . . .

Liam Macleod (9)
Muirtown Primary School, Inverness

Feeling Lonely

Standing in the playground
Watching people play,
Feeling invisible
Day after day,
All by myself.
Suddenly the bell,
I walk in slowly,
Get changed quietly,
Go up to class
And wait for the teacher to come.

Avie Sutherland (9)
Muirtown Primary School, Inverness

Just Me

I am in the playground
All on my own,
Not one person wants
To play with me.
I hear the bell
And walk to the classroom,
Thinking what it
Would be like
To have friends.

Rhuary MacDougall (10)
Muirtown Primary School, Inverness

All Alone

Sitting in the classroom,
Sitting on my own,
Nobody to talk to.
The teacher just stares,
People always laugh at me,
I sadly and slowly walk out of the class
Dreading the next day to come.

Ciara Polson (9)
Muirtown Primary School, Inverness

Untitled

I like to ride my bike,
I like to go very fast
Because it is a blast.

I have a pet cat,
She is a bit of a brat,
She swings on the curtains!

Connor Munro (10)
Muirtown Primary School, Inverness

I Am All Alone

Standing in the playground
Watching people play
Watching them for hours
Every single day
I am standing there
Standing in the rain
I wish that some people would come over and play
I wish I could play
Every game in the world.

Morven Macdonald (9)
Muirtown Primary School, Inverness

My Best Friend

She smells like daffodils,
She is a spicy curry,
She's a fizzy lemon,
She is snowy as winter,
She's a bright yellow,
She's always sunny,
She's as cool as me,
She's a good singer
And she is my best friend.

Kerri Whyte (10)
Our Lady of Peace Primary School, Paisley

My Teacher

He's a chatting, mad monkey,
He's a cool November's day,
He's a bright, golden sun,
He smells of grapefruit in the morning,
He's a soft red chair,
He's a floating golden chip,
The sound of singing children!

Paul Flannigan (10)
Our Lady of Peace Primary School, Paisley

My Best Friend

She's a jumping jack,
She's a happy hyena,
She's a little mouse,
She's as bright as the sun,
She's a kind little teddy bear,
She's a pair of chatting jaws,
She's the smell of rosy flowers.

Frankie Barrett (10)
Our Lady of Peace Primary School, Paisley

My Best Friend

She's a quiet girl,
She's a bright delight,
She's fit and slim,
She's always on the move,
She's a busy girl, very cool,
She's the smell of rosy flowers,
She's the shape of a skinny pop star,
She's a very good singer - better than me,
But will always be my best friend.

Kelly-Anne McDougall (10)
Our Lady of Peace Primary School, Paisley

My Best Friend

She's a bright sun,
A giggling, chattering monkey,
A fizzy cup of lemonade,
The smell of roses in the summer,
The sun showers in winter,
She's my best friend,
She's Kate.

Emma Cunningham (10)
Our Lady of Peace Primary School, Paisley

My Friend Kirsty

She's a fizzy wizzy witch,
She's a furry wurry teddy,
She's a furry dog,
She's a book full of information,
She's a big red apple,
She's a good girl, sometimes!
She's a bright yellow sun,
She's a boxing kangaroo,
She's as soft as a butterfly.

Ellese McInalty (10)
Our Lady of Peace Primary School, Paisley

My Mum

She smells like roses,
She is kind as a puppy,
She is smart as a businessman,
She opens like a door,
She's a fizzy drink,
She's a good singer,
She's a bouncy chair,
She's waking up and having a sharp shower.

Kerry Docherty (10)
Our Lady of Peace Primary School, Paisley

My Friend Shannon Delaney

She's a bright yellow sun,
She's a soft fluffy pillow,
A snowman standing still,
A crazy monkey,
A bouncy kangaroo,
The sound of singing,
The sun in June,
A dancing queen.

Shona Strachan (10)
Our Lady of Peace Primary School, Paisley

My Best Friend

She is bright as the sun in the summer,
She is a sudden barking dog,
She is friendly like a baby,
She is active like a running dog,
She is tough as nails,
She is sparkly like a can of Coke,
She is chatty like swinging monkeys,
She is smart like Mr Stewart,
She is cheeky like monkeys,
She is a cuddly teddy bear, always there to cuddle,
She is caring like my mum,
She is a bright red door always open,
She is happy like the sun.

Chloe Gorton (10)
Our Lady of Peace Primary School, Paisley

My Brother

He's a fluffy teddy,
He's a bouncy chair,
He's a spicy curry,
He's a bright orange door left open,
The smell of daffodils,
He's a growly old bear,
He's a bright red sun,
He's a smart lion,
He's a tall giraffe,
A fizzy drink,
A magic magician.

Seona Kelly (10)
Our Lady of Peace Primary School, Paisley

My Brothers, David And Michael

My brother David thinks he's really cool,
But really to me he's a big, big fool,
He says things about me to all of his friends,
Will his cruelty never end?
Sometimes he is in my dreams,
He makes me want to get up and scream.

My little brother is just the same,
He may be little but he's really a pain,
They both want to go to the swimming pool,
But if you look at them you'll know that they're cruel,
After all that, I suppose I can say,
I suppose they are pretty OK in a way.

Sarah Smith (10)
Port Elphinstone Primary School, Inverurie

Ice Cream

Ice cream is delicious and sweet,
Different flavours, good to eat,
Freezing teeth and freezing feet,
With chocolate sauce it is a treat.

Ice cream in tubs and cones,
Enough to freeze all your bones,
Gulp it, lick it, swallow fast,
Now it's gone, it didn't last!

Laura Jaffray (8)
Port Elphinstone Primary School, Inverurie

The Old Scarecrow

There was an old scarecrow
Who loved to dance,
To twirl and spin
And hop and prance.

He loved to scare the birds away,
Away from the crops,
Away from the hay.

In the field, watch him grow,
And then you can say,
What a jolly scarecrow!

Rachel Murray (9)
Port Elphinstone Primary School, Inverurie

My Teddy

My teddy is brown and soft
I found him lying in the loft
He's dusty, tattered and torn,
I've had him since the day I was born.

My grandma fixed him,
Cleaned his fur,
Sewed his patches
And made him purr!

Dean Sockalingum (9)
Port Elphinstone Primary School, Inverurie

Four Sisters

I have four sisters,
In case you didn't know,
Let's start with Kayleigh
And go! Go! Go!

She picks her toes,
She makes a mess,
When I have friends in
She is just a pest!

Now let's get on with Chloe,
She really is a clown,
Whenever she is playing,
She turns the room upside down!

Now Hannah and Eve are twins,
They are really rather cute,
They give me hugs and kisses,
But at night they turn into witches!

And now there's to be another!
Will it be girl or boy?
Another one to annoy me,
I wish they would leave me alone!

Lauren McGhee (10)
Port Elphinstone Primary School, Inverurie

Fred The Teddy

Fred the teddy is my friend,
He's really cute and soft,
I like to take him to my bed
And cuddle him at night.

I talk to him when I'm angry,
I talk to him when I'm sad,
I cuddle him when I'm frightened,
I hit him when I'm mad.

Jamie Fenty (9)
Port Elphinstone Primary School, Inverurie

The Trolls' Day Out

Today's the day when the trolls go out
They'll be up to no good without a doubt
Sneaking in houses, stealing the food,
Prowling through the trees in the depths of the wood.
Climbing up mountains, swimming through seas
Frightening everyone and being a tease!

Matthew Gillies (8)
Port Elphinstone Primary School, Inverurie

My Pet Cat

My pet cat thinks he's the best,
Even better than all the rest,
He jumps, fights and runs around,
He even rolls upon the ground.
For you that might not be much,
But for my family he is such
A son to my mother,
A grandson to my grandparents,
For us he is the best, the best pet there is.

Nadia Warner (8)
Port Elphinstone Primary School, Inverurie

Dolphins

Dolphins splish and dolphins splash,
Going past in a flash.
Having fun and leaping high,
Trying to reach the sky.
Twisting, turning in the sea,
Won't you come and swim with me.

Melissa Morrice (9)
Port Elphinstone Primary School, Inverurie

Boys And Girls

Boys are cool,
Boys are smart,
Boys rule,
They get the part,

Girls are cool,
Girls are smart,
Girls pull,
They steal your heart.

William Mutch (10)
Port Elphinstone Primary School, Inverurie

Waiting

Cold, damp, never-ending, hollow tunnel,
Battering waves crashing against the barnacle-encrusted rocks,
Misty, overcast sky thundering overhead,
As they stand anxiously, in pain!

Gary Pullar (11)
Ravenswood Primary School, Cumbernauld

A Small Dot

A small dot,
A slithery tot.

A little hisser,
A poisoned kisser.

A rattle keeper,
A mouse reaper.

A stripy rake,
To make a *snake!*

Lori-Jaye Hooks (11)
Ravenswood Primary School, Cumbernauld

Fireworks

F ierce Ferris wheel flies flamboyantly,
I gnite indulgent indigo illusions,
R aining red rockets,
E merald energy, exploding everywhere,
W hacky whistling wails,
O range outbursts overhead,
R apidly racing rubies,
K ung fu kaleidoscope
S izzling sapphire stars.

Adam Jenkins (11)
Ravenswood Primary School, Cumbernauld

A Cat

Bird-chaser,
sly-seeker,

milk-drinker,
mouse-killer,

bush-hider,
knee-warmer,

high-pouncer,
hard-purrer,

fish-eater,
face-scratcher,

balanced-walker,
long-jumper.

A cat!

Amy Allan (11)
Ravenswood Primary School, Cumbernauld

Fireworks

F abulous, flashing, falling fireworks
I deal, impressive, illusions
R ushing, rockets, rapidly rising
E xploding, enormous, entertainment
W histling, white, whining wail
O utside, overhead, occasion
R evolting, ridiculous rockets
K icking, killing kaleidoscopes
S parkling, swooping, sizzling stars.

Alastair Stephen (12)
Ravenswood Primary School, Cumbernauld

Trapped

Powerful, deadly waves crash against the crooked stack,
Jagged rocks crumble into the sea,
A steep, bottomless gorge fills the stack,
Massive waves crash their tiny boat,
The hollow stack.

Christopher Reid (11)
Ravenswood Primary School, Cumbernauld

War

The black, dark nights where bombs fall,
Through the sky like fireflies,
Sparkling, shooting stars light up the sky,
Dusty smoke and the burning of wood fills my nose,
Screaming terror!
The fear consumes all!
Crashes and explosions hurt my ears.
Bitter and sour it almost melts my soul,
This is a bloodthirsty
War!

Louise Donaldson (11)
Ravenswood Primary School, Cumbernauld

The Bomb

Black like dried out veins,
Blown up volcano, *sizzle, sizzle,*
Houses fall on the bumpy, rocky road,
Blazing, bubbling fireballs,
Smoky forest, burning high,
Stacked rubbish, sizzling away,
Earth exploding at our door,
Electricity burning freely.

Hollie Lang (11)
Ravenswood Primary School, Cumbernauld

The Stack

Towering stack became increasingly closer.
Ocean took children by incredible force.
Bloodthirsty waves swept madly through
The dark, dull, hollow stack.
Dark, overcast sky, flashed and boomed overhead.
Dark, scary, haunted tunnels, never-ending.
Terrified children felt so lonely,
They felt ghostly spirits following them.
Both struggled on and on.

Scott Girvan (11)
Ravenswood Primary School, Cumbernauld

The Stack

Fierce, strong waves,
Barge past strong, solid rocks,
Cold, dark, damp caves,
Scared, nervous children
Travel on.

Chloe Rice (11)
Ravenswood Primary School, Cumbernauld

Music

Blue as the sky,
Peace and joy,
Loud as drums,
Sweet as sugar,
Like a rose,
Like a family,
Just want to play for fun,
Soft as a fluffy ball,
Bright lighted concerts.

Stefan Weir (11)
Ravenswood Primary School, Cumbernauld

Fireworks

F abulous, falling, flickering flares,
I ncredible, inspiring images,
R acing rockets, rapidly roaring,
E xciting, exploding entertainment,
W hooshing whirls whizzing,
O dd, outside occasion,
R ushing rockets rage,
K icking, killing kaleidoscope,
S tars swooping seriously.

Amy Lightfoot (11)
Ravenswood Primary School, Cumbernauld

Rain

Blue like the sky,
Cold, damp sea,
Pitter-patter of tiny feet,
Freezing cold water,
Teardrops falling,
Little, tiny blue balls.

Jennifer Ward (11)
Ravenswood Primary School, Cumbernauld

The Young Lady In Red

There was a young lady in red,
She only ate butter and bread,
She messed up her dress,
Right through to her vest,
That silly young lady in red.

Rebecca Redmond (11)
Ravenswood Primary School, Cumbernauld

Hatred

Black as the night,
Thunderbolts whacking the cornfield,
Sirens wailing and screaming,
Fizzing sour sherbet,
Mountains of disgusting rubbish,
A room of deadly axes and chainsaws,
A sharp bed of nails,
A shooting pain right through your heart,
Falling into a bush of nettles.

David McMeeking (11)
Ravenswood Primary School, Cumbernauld

The Storm

Thundering, crashing waves bang against the hard rocks,
Stormy, black sea crashes against the stack,
Big, dark tunnel drips of water,
Inside all damp, hollow and silent.
Children fearful of what they might meet,
Along the silent, scary, deadly way of the stack.

Danielle Hall (11)
Ravenswood Primary School, Cumbernauld

Love

Deep pink like a fluffy pillow,
Chocolate melting in your mouth,
Flowers blooming in the sunshine,
The sweet scent of roses,
A golden harp playing,
Butterflies dancing in your tummy.

Rebecca Taylor (11)
Ravenswood Primary School, Cumbernauld

Fireworks

F lashing, fancy flares,
I ncredible, impulsive illusion,
R acing rockets rapidly rushing,
E xploding, exciting entertainment,
W histling, whizzing whines,
O utside observing overhead,
R ushing, racing rocket,
K illing, kicking kaleidoscope,
S izzling, swooping stars.

Ryan Hendrie (11)
Ravenswood Primary School, Cumbernauld

The Bomb

Black like a dried out heart,
Your hands crumbling before your eyes,
Soldiers giving up their lives for you,
Gravestones falling apart,
Forests and houses burning and crackling like mad,
A red rose bursting and dying,
Your tongue falls off with a horrible taste,
Burning flames and melting pieces.
Bomb!

Heather Speedie (11)
Ravenswood Primary School, Cumbernauld

The Stack

Fierce, terrifying waves,
Viciously battered
Against jagged rocks.
Deadly, high waves swept madly
Through the dark, dull, hollow stack.
Blood-red sky!
Battered, bruised children carry on,
Through the deadly, terrifying stack.

Mark Adams (11)
Ravenswood Primary School, Cumbernauld

The Lady From Spain

There once was a lady from Spain,
Who fell off a very large plane,
She broke her spine,
But now she's fine
The next time she'll go on a train!

Gavin Rae (11)
Ravenswood Primary School, Cumbernauld

Darkness

Black like a wet, dark tunnel,
Empty space with nobody in sight,
Lonely with a murky, moonless sky,
Horrible, dark chocolate,
Cold-hearted ghosts,
Horrible, musty, wet ground.

Darkness!

Steven Harvie (11)
Ravenswood Primary School, Cumbernauld

Death

Black like the Grim Reaper's coat,
The Grim Reaper calling for you,
Blood trickling down your tongue,
The stench of rotten corpses,
A grave where you will lie forever,
Touch of Death's finger,
About to drop dead,
Rest in peace!

Michael Stewart (11)
Ravenswood Primary School, Cumbernauld

Ladybird Haikus

Lovely ladybird
Darling dancer, sweet as pie,
Elegant creature.

Ladybird so sweet,
ladybird so delicate,
So aerobatic.

Ladybird so young,
You are so intelligent,
You are a flower.

Your squeak is so soft,
Your wings are so delicate,
Like sugar paper.

Sweetness is your life,
For you are so beautiful,
Just like a flower.

Janet Mary Provan (8)
St Leonards School, St Andrews

Worm

Wiggly worm like a long piece of string
Wriggling through the mud
Thinking,
I am a dirty worm
Happily squelching in my playful mud.

Oliver Rogers-Jones (8)
St Leonards School, St Andrews

Snails

Deep down in the roots of the great tree,
A snail lives,
Hazelnut-like house carried upon his back.
Sausage body, rolls out of his shell,
Solitary snail deep down in the roots of
The great tree.

Oliver de Mountfalcon (9)
St Leonards School, St Andrews

Blue-Black Beetle

The ground beetle groans
As he creeps and crawls along the ground
Blue-black, back as hard as metal
Jaggy as a holly tree
Every spike like a sharp needle
He doesn't know where he is going
Poor ground beetle.

Jonathan Blackburn (9)
St Leonards School, St Andrews

The Horribly Hairy House Spider

I am only a house spider,
Searching for a home,
But to humans I am just a horribly hairy house spider.

I mean no harm,
Just a crack will do,
But to humans I am just a horribly hairy house spider.

I don't take up much room,
Behind a sink is fine,
But to humans I am just a horribly hairy house spider.

I am more scared of you than you are of me,
My webs are fairly big, but there's only room for one,
But to humans I am just a horribly hairy house spider.

I have finally found a home
With someone who doesn't mind,
To him I am *not* a horribly hairy house spider.

Robert Clark (10)
St Leonards School, St Andrews

Rickety Red Insects

Rickety, red insects
Tomato-red they breathe out hot air
Like a cockroach they scare you
Red lizards eating red flies
But they don't eat red tarantulas
They are too scared.

Small green frog
Croaking happily on a huge, green lily pad
Deep in his head his eyes
Look for food.
Green trees, green grass
And green insects.

Callum Morse (8)
St Leonards School, St Andrews

Creepy-Crawly Friends

Fragrance of flowers
Fluttering feather-like princess
Hovering like a multicoloured helicopter
Shining dress shaking over the leaf
Tottering, topsy-turvy, long-legged princess
Balancing lightly
Lovely, beautiful ballroom dancing butterfly
Fairy, fizzing and fluttering
Everyone's friend.

Friend of ladybird
Who is like a tiny, red and black tortoise
Shining in the sizzling sun
Like a freshly cleaned doorknob
Glowing
She splits in half to fly
To visit her best butterfly friend

Snake slithering, sliding
Shining with a tongue
As red as Jupiter's hot spot
Robin Hood's arrow
Dancing a waltz
Trying to find a friend too.

Bethany Ferguson (8)
St Leonards School, St Andrews

Fly

Paper wings spinning
Body like an apple pip
Small, hard and oval-shaped
Bungee-jumping round my house
Eyes like pinheads
Curiously looking for a dead mouse
To munch on
For his luncheon!

Elizabeth Clark (8)
St Leonards School, St Andrews

The Spider And The Fly

Licking his lips
Spider saw Fly passing by.
'What a fine web you have,' wickedly said Fly
Not noticing the menace in the sky,
'You don't scare me at all.'
Too late . . .
Swooping through the air
Spider fired his web
Caught the fly
Struggling while the spider wrapped him
Round and round
And round and round
Into a solid white cocoon
Spider's dinner.

Andrew Taylor (9)
St Leonards School, St Andrews

The Snake

Slimy, slithering snake,
Naughty, noisy snake like a jumbo elephant trunk.
Snoring snake,
Curled up waiting for some food.
Suddenly unfurling like a spring.
Jumping for joy.
Pouncing on a baby mouse.
Like a drainpipe rope
He sucks it all in
Squirming down his throat and eats it all up.

Rebecca Mackay (8)
St Leonards School, St Andrews

Bees

The worker bee's pollination
Pays off at the end of the day
When the queen bee rewards him
With his first taste of honey
Which is like the first bud of spring
Or the first snowfall.

But what they don't know is
That tomorrow the beekeeper
Is going to take it all away,
Bottle it and sell it all
And make his fortune
All in one day.

He is the masked, evil one
He wears a net and white suit
It is heavy and thick
We try to fight him off
But he always wins.
Our stings do not affect
The masked, evil one.

Olivia Gibson (9)
St Leonards School, St Andrews

My Insect Friend

I have a friend
An insect friend
Who frolics free in my garden
He's an imaginary bug
Who stands up on two feet
Black as the night sky
Big, bad beetle
Plays with me.

Oliver Hazell (9)
St Leonards School, St Andrews

The Lobster And The Tadpole

Lobster sitting on the bottom of the sea
Sighed,
'I'm so lonely, I need a friend.'
Far away in a river a tadpole said,
'I'm so lonely, I need someone to talk to.'
They met in a river and became firm friends
Until . . .
One sunny day
Tadpole looked down, expecting a black, silky skin
But he was all green
And a frog!
'You look funny today, Tadpole,' laughed Lobster,
'I've got a frog friend now.'

Jordan Hutchison (8)
St Leonards School, St Andrews

Wasp

Lanky, striped body like a football strip.
Delicate, cracked wings, like frosted glass.
Thin, tiny legs like silk threads,
The wasp waits in his nest.

Fast, slick movements like a tiny bird.
Buzzing, purring like an expensive car.
Swooping down on the garden beds,
The wasp sits on the flower.

Turning, staring like a soldier on guard,
Watching, looking like a cheetah hunting,
Scaring the children who sit on the grass,
The wasp springs on his prey.

David Mackay (9)
St Leonards School, St Andrews

Bluebottle

Honeycomb eyes
Sly, buzzing bluebottle
Smelling like old water
Making a lot of noise
Buzzing fuzzily against the window
Bouncing frantically at the glass
Trying to get out into the world.

Bang! Bang! Bang!
Dodging right and left.
The clashing, thrashing swat
Fly, fly up high
Trying to get into the world.

Holly Milne (9)
St Leonards School, St Andrews

Wiggly Worm

I don't know what to do.
I'm all twisted up, in a muddle,
In a puddle up to my middle,
On a beautiful summer's day.

Wriggle, wriggle tiny worm,
In your tunnels
Oozing and wiggling all day.
How weird,
You are working so hard.

Nina Duncan (9)
St Leonards School, St Andrews

Caterpillar To Butterfly

I once caught a tiny caterpillar,
It was really neat,
Even if it was very slow,
It still was my best friend,
But lately, I don't know.

Lately it's been terribly busy,
Always scurrying around,
My mum said,
'It's probably building a cocoon.'
I wish I could play.

It went inside its new, fresh home,
I thought it would come out again
I waited and waited, tears rolling down my cheeks
But no, he had left me,
I miss him, I want him.

'He's out! He's out!'
I screamed with joy,
But what met my tear-filled eyes?
I was horrified but thrilled at the same time
A beautiful butterfly fluttering silently about.

Katie Overend (9)
St Leonards School, St Andrews

Obstacle Course

Obstacle course of sticks and leaves
A maze of jaggy, giant grass and muddy puddles.
Moving like a pebble being skimmed across the sea
Legs like extra thin icicles
Slowly the spider struggles to reach the end.

I see a speck of illuminated dust
As the sun catches his web.
Death happens suddenly
To the fly caught in the patterned spiral threads.

Hannah Gray (9)
St Leonards School, St Andrews

Spider Terror

Not everyone is scared of spiders.
Let us start with the really terrifying ones.

Shelob poisons, guts and eats her victims,
She lives at the edge of Mordor
Eating slimy, tough orcs.
But when Frodo intruded into her lair
His elven light drove her back.

Aragog waits eagerly for her victims
To come unsuspecting into her
Dark and shadowy cave.
But Harry and Ron,
When they were trapped
With spiders all around,
Were saved by Weasley's flying car.

Paraosa lugubris, thought to lurk
Beyond our shores,
Now lives in Scotland!
She feeds by pouncing on
And devouring her prey
But don't worry,
She's only five millimetres long!

Richard Ward (10)
St Leonards School, St Andrews

Happy Snappy

Happy, snappy scorpion,
Strolling along the scorching desert,
Stinging tail, full of poison.
Nippy crab-like claws,
Fangs as strong as rocks,
Happily strolling back to his burrow,
After demolishing a cricket.

Jaimie Morse (9)
St Leonards School, St Andrews

I Am A Spider

I am a spider,
A friendly spider.
I don't know why people run away
When they see me.

I am a spider,
A friendly spider.
Some people pick me up
And care for me.

I am a spider,
A friendly spider.
I think I know why people run away,
They are scared of me.

To be honest,
I am scared of them.
I am a spider,
A friendly spider.

Ged Rutherford (10)
St Leonards School, St Andrews

Haiku On A Butterfly

Shimmering creature,
The bright butterfly, bobbing
Silently searching.

Tabitha Gordon-Smith (8)
St Leonards School, St Andrews

Firefly

Sounding like the whistle of the wind,
I am the goddess of fireflies,
Golden butter-like ring on my back,
I am scared of the dark
So I keep my light on.
Glowing warm, a golden angel.
Soft light, like Heaven's door has been opened.
Weeping inky, golden drops of light,
I fly through the night.

Jasmine Wilson (10)
St Leonards School, St Andrews

Wriggling Worm

Like a long piece of spaghetti
The clever worm's wriggling his way across the garden
Momentarily stopping for a break
Looking round at the wibbly wobbly world.

Dark and watery, squashy mud
Tunnelling through the squelchy soil
Searching, searching for a nice, new home,
Underneath the gooey garden
Goes the wriggling worm.

Keir Hunter (9)
St Leonards School, St Andrews

My Poem About A Butterfly

Eggies, eggies,
When will you hatch?
Do you think that you will match
Your other brothers?

Eggies, eggies,
You're beginning to hatch,
That's great, now whom do you match?
Do you match your sisters or your brothers
Come on tell me, any others?

Caterpillar, caterpillar,
What are you doing?
Are you eating
Delicious leaves?

Caterpillar, caterpillar,
You are getting fatter,
Does shedding your skins matter?

Caterpillar, caterpillar,
You're wrapping silk around yourself.
Is the plant a type of shelf?

Cocoon, cocoon,
I've been waiting two weeks
For you to hatch,
To see if you like leeks.

Butterfly, butterfly,
You're out of the cocoon,
Wait a little while
And your wings will dry soon.

Butterfly, butterfly,
It's time for you to flutter by
So *bye!*

Rebecca Taylor (10)
St Leonards School, St Andrews

The Centipede

Deep, deep, deep in the forest
There lived a centipede
But this centipede was special
Cos he had a missing wee leg
So he tried and tried
For that missing wee leg
But he never got it you see.

So he consulted his friend Meg
About his missing wee leg
And his friend said,
'Just don't worry,
Anyway what's the hurry?
We've got the rest of the day,' she said.

Meg was a millipede
With a thousand wee legs you see.
'Meg,' he whispered,
'Mmm!'
'Can I borrow one of your legs?'
'No!' she exclaimed.
'But isn't 999 enough?'
'No!' she said in an instant,
'You have 99 and that's tough.'

But the next time she saw him
He looked rather dashin'
With a smile on his face
Cos he'd started a fashion
Of having a missing wee leg
So trendy and smashin'
Meg was distraught
For she never had thought
That too many legs she'd be flashin'!

Cameron Spencer (10)
St Leonards School, St Andrews

Shy Yet Warrior

Woodlouse
Potato bug
Warrior bug
Slayer.

Looks like a tough,
Strong, threatening warrior
Padded with
Strong, defensive armour
But as shy as a mouse.

It feels like the leather on
The front of your boot.
It senses danger,
Such a sensitive creature.

Small yet big
It rapidly scuttles under a log.
Silence but the sound of lightly
Pattering feet,
Cautious but curious
As it scuttles up the pipe,
A scream in the bath, an
Unnecessary fright!

Flora Ogilvy (10)
St Leonards School, St Andrews

Beautiful Bug

Friendly butterfly, beautiful bug,
Shaped wings like an angel's,
Little lady, not a bug,
Travels from place to place.
Green, white and red,
Fly smoothly in the air
And lands lightly on the flowers.

Emilie Chalmers (11)
St Leonards School, St Andrews

A Millipede

Red scales under ragged rocks,
Energised to scuttle far from sight.
Sleeping
In dingy and damp cracks.
Sensitive spokes, like spidery stacks,
Elongated to
Unite the legs.
Long feelers for
Foraging
In dingy and damp cracks.

Adam Harris (11)
St Leonards School, St Andrews

Just A Normal Caterpillar

I am a caterpillar,
Just a normal caterpillar,
But I don't think I should live.
All I do is eat and eat,
There's nothing for me in this big world.

I am a caterpillar,
Just a normal caterpillar,
But I don't think I should live.
All of my friends are good at something,
Everyone but me,
I am useless . . .

Josh Jamieson (11)
St Leonards School, St Andrews

Creepy-Crawly School

On Monday morning, just like you and me,
All the little bugs are waking in their trees,
Now they're ready to go!
They've packed away their school bags,
Pencil cases and all!

When the bell goes
Everyone knows that school has begun.
Mrs Bethany the butterfly comes out to greet everyone.
'Good morning school, now settle down,
Let's try our
Hardest for today, no need to growl or frown!'

First up is maths with Mrs Wendy the worm,
She's very slow the dear old thing,
Never up for a dance or a fling!
Second, English, Mrs Cryer the caterpillar takes this class,
She talks very fast!

Out in the playground,
All the older bugs like Max the mosquito,
Are picking on other bugs,
Like poor old Beatrice the bumblebee, when . . .
Bang!
She stings them with her sharp little end,
I think Max won't want *her* as his friend!

So it's nearly time to go back home
And everyone is very tired.
By their teachers quite inspired.
Tomorrow is another day, a fresh start.
In the morning they will get up
And get all dressed again smart!

Alice Ferguson (11)
St Leonards School, St Andrews

A Mum In A Million

My mum is a mum in a million,
She takes notice of all that I do
And when there are days when I'm feeling sad
She says, 'Nicolle, I will be there for you.'

No matter if she's feeling happy,
No matter if she's feeling sad,
There is always one thing she says and it's,
'You're the best friend I've ever had.'

Nicolle Briggs (11)
St Mary's Primary School, Maryhill

My Little Cousin Sean

My little cousin Sean is a cute little boy,
He has a cuddly reindeer which is his favourite toy.

Every time I see him he always laughs,
He likes playing with his toys in his baths.

Every time I play with him we have lots of fun,
I can't wait till he grows up, until he can run.

I love little babies but Sean is like no other,
Instead of being my cousin I wish he was my brother!

Alexander McIntosh (11)
St Mary's Primary School, Maryhill

Do I Have Two Faces?

Look in the mirror, what do you see?
Do you see you there or do you see me?
I can't really see my reflection
But when the mirror is fixed
I will still ask myself,
Do I have two faces?

Danielle Brown (11)
St Mary's Primary School, Maryhill

My Tiger Sister

My tiger sister is always on the prowl,
If you don't give her what she wants
She gives you a sly growl.

She goes in bad moods and jumps
Up and down before she falls.
Although she's only two
Her scream echoes through you.

Even though she's a menace,
I still love her to bits.

Leanne Monaghan (11)
St Mary's Primary School, Maryhill

Snow

Snow is wonderful,
Snow is great,
Snow is like ice cream on a plate.
Snow is cold,
It makes you shiver,
It ices up on the river.
When it snows, the wind blows
And makes your nose go red as a rose.

Shelley Burke & Eilidh MacNeill (10)
St Mary's Primary School, Maryhill

My Dad

My dad, he makes me glad,
My dad, he makes me laugh all day.
My dad likes to say jokes,
My dad pokes me to make me laugh,
My dad helps me with my maths homework,
I love my dad and he loves me.

Kerry Spence (11)
St Mary's Primary School, Maryhill

My Cat

He prowls around the house
Before he plays with his toy mouse.
He licks his lips when my mum is
Making his favourite meal.
He may be hyper or sometimes sad . . .
But he is never bad.
He likes to jump around the house
While I am cleaning
And he also loves to be the centre of attention,
He is just a big softie who likes all his toffee.
He is my cat . . . but I am proud of him,
He is my cat, Breezer.

Lauren Grieve (11)
St Mary's Primary School, Maryhill

I'm Bored

I hate being bored.
When my toys get broken,
I leave them alone.
Then I sit on my own,
Thinking they're broken.
When I wake up on Sunday morning
Nothing's on TV but BB3B
I hate going into town
Because I never get to buy things.
In a shop I'm always hungry.
Being bad annoys my dad
And I get in a mood.

Kieran Wilkie (8)
St Peter's RC Primary School, Aberdeen

Playground Games

Playground games are lots of fun,
When it's bright with lots of sun.
A girl is skipping with a rope,
And boys and girls are playing 'tig and tag'.
Balls are bouncing,
Kids are screaming,
Laughing and crying,
Crunching, screaming.
Gates that rattle,
Trees that creak
Above the din, we hear the bell
Dina-a-ling!
Time to go in.

Toni-Marie Wharry (8)
St Peter's RC Primary School, Aberdeen

Playground

People in the playground,
Children in the playground,
Adults in the playground.
Hoops in the playground,
Ropes in the playground,
Basically everything in the playground.
Now it's winter and
I've got those playground blues.
The teachers, they're sitting inside in the warm,
Drinking gallons of coffee.
Oh, I wish I were a teacher,
But for now I've got those cold playtime blues.

I love school and I've no more playtime blues!

Dario Giuseppe Piedipalumbo (8)
St Peter's RC Primary School, Aberdeen

My Playground

My playground is boring,
There is nothing to do
Except skipping
Skip-a-doodle-loo
And I've got those cold playtime blues.

My playground is boring,
I'm freezing out here!
My friend is next to me shivering,
To an ice cube like me!
And I've got those cold playtime blues.

My playground is boring,
Everything is all dull.
No birds are singing at all,
I wish I was inside, all cosy and warm,
And I've still
Got those cold playtime blues.

My playground is boring,
I've nobody to play with
They're just standing like ice cubes,
Now it starts to rain.
And guess what I've still got?
Those cold playtime blues.

It's spring today,
I see the daffodils growing,
The birds singing songs
All the children playing
And I've finally got rid of . . .
Those cold playtime blues!

Bronach Boyle (8)
St Peter's RC Primary School, Aberdeen

I Went To Investigate

I saw this thing in the garden,
The phone rang, ting-a-ling,
Picked it up, the school asked me to sing!
Went to school, saw this thing,
I went to investigate . . .

It was the king's crown!
I gave it to the teacher, she wore it when I sang.
I had to wear a fang, I was a vampire!
Got home, it rained, I slipped in a puddle,
Got really wet, saw something in the puddle,
I went to investigate . . .

It was a tutu, I gave it to the teacher,
She wore it when I danced,
I had to wear clown's pants!
When I got home it was sunny,
I saw this thing, a weird shadow,
I went to investigate . . .

It was really high-heeled shoes!
I gave them to the teacher,
She wore them when I told her jokes.
I had to wear a pink, glittery dress
With flowers all over it.
Got home, it was windy, my skirt flew up,
I was starting to blush.
Then my dad saw me!
He laughed his head off . . .
I didn't go to investigate!

Jaime Robb (8)
St Peter's RC Primary School, Aberdeen

Dog In The Playground

Dog in the playground,
Jumping through the air.
I know that dog
He belongs to the Mayor!

Dog in the playground
Playing with me
I know its name. It's Rob.

Dog in the playground,
Just suddenly there.
Dog in the playground
Make a bit of a fuss.
Dog in the playground
Playing with us.
I know that dog, he lives next door to me!

Dog in the playground,
Always around us.

Parham Tadayon (8)
St Peter's RC Primary School, Aberdeen

Playtime

Yeah! It's playtime,
I feel like having some fun.
I don't know what to do,
Oh, that game looks fun.
I'll go and ask if I can join in.
Screaming and shouting,
Angry drivers beeping their horns,
Police cars chasing burglars,
Ambulances rushing to hospital.
All of a sudden the bell has gone,
Time to line up and go inside!

Lauren Baxter (9)
St Peter's RC Primary School, Aberdeen

Playground Blues

I've got those cold playtime blues,
My feet are cold,
My feet are wet,
I want my mummy
But I mustn't fret.
I'm soaking wet,
I'm all alone,
I'm cold right to the bone.
And I've got those cold playtime blues.

I've got nowhere to hide,
I can't stay inside
And I've got those cold playtime blues.

I haven't got anyone to talk to
Or to play with,
And after all that waiting -
There goes the whistle
And I'm out of those cold playtime blues!

Eden Johnson (8)
St Peter's RC Primary School, Aberdeen

Fun Playground

Fun playground, sometimes worse,
Fun playground, sometimes better,
Some people are skipping, jumping,
Walking, talking,
But I'm always left alone!

The only friend I have is my *imaginary friend!*
And she never ever lets me down,
And my friends always say,
'Who are you talking to?'
But *we* know who I'm talking to -
Don't we?

Chipego Siamuwele (8)
St Peter's RC Primary School, Aberdeen

Busy Girl

I like playing but I have no time.
My friends keep asking,
 'Do you want to play?'
And I say I would love to, but I have no time.
Sometimes I can play, but look what happened!

I was skipping and Mat was skipping,
But he could only skip once, so he cried in the playground.
I wanted to be kind, so I said, 'Are you okay?'
'I'm fine, can you help me?'
So I said, 'Okay!' and I helped him.
But I couldn't stand it because no one else helped him.
I asked my friend,
We all played with happiness,
And played a lot.

Shannen Katerina Romero-Pérez (8)
St Peter's RC Primary School, Aberdeen

Children In The Playground

Children playing having fun,
Children joking, laughing loud.
Children tigging, playing a game,
Children coming, children going.
Children running, having a race.
Children dancing round and round.
Children drawing with the chalk,
Children leaping, playing leapfrog.
Children playing with dolls.
Children playing with a frisbee.
Children jogging around the playground.
Children reading, reading for school,
Children falling, now crying
And some children do absolutely nothing.

Matthew Ross (8)
St Peter's RC Primary School, Aberdeen

Children In The Playground

Children jumping,
Children skipping,
Children running,
Children kicking.
Children screaming,
Children leaping,
Maybe even more!

Rolling about, soaring about,
Boring about, some in hoops
Some in groups,
Some around the playground door.
In the sand, on a rope,
All around the playground.

On a chair, on a bench,
What's the difference, at the fence?
Playtime is coming to an end and
So my friend, the playground is a lovely place
Full of fun and lots of space.

Jack Alexander (8)
St Peter's RC Primary School, Aberdeen

Playground

Children are playing,
The whistle's just gone.
Children lining up,
Now it's playtime.
Children joking and playing,
Children jumping and running,
Children drawing and skipping,
Children playing tie and tag and racing.
Children reading, ready for church,
Children crying and laughing.

Shalin Abraham (8)
St Peter's RC Primary School, Aberdeen

The Playground, The Playground

The playground, the playground,
Here I come every day.
Run, skip, hop, jump and play.

The playground, the playground,
On a sunny day, I feel lots of energy.
It's such fun in the sun.
Planting seeds, playing with beads.

The playground, the playground,
You can play tie 'n' tag, take a ball out of a bag.
Sit down, stand up. What am I talking about?

The playground, the playground
It's windy, I'll play with my friend Cindy.
On a cold wet day, I get so sad and mad.
I wish it would just stop and go plop!
When there's fog, I want to jog and stop!

The playground, the playground,
It's so fine, don't forget to stand in line.
Someone falls and hurts their knee,
'Ouch!' I got stung by a bee.

The playground, the playground,
You have to wait till the whistle blows,
Can't go inside, even if it snows.

The playground, the playground,
I can hear tummies rumbling,
Children stumbling towards the dinner hall.

Nicole Anderson (8)
St Peter's RC Primary School, Aberdeen

Playtime

When it's playtime,
We all go out,
Filing out, piling out.

Then it's playtime
Some run around,
Skipping or chasing a ball,
Bawling and falling and having a fit.

Walking or talking,
Tigging and tagging.
Oh no! I'm it!
Hiding-and-seeking and crying too,
Shouting and screaming
It's a hullabaloo
When it's playtime.

Clyde Hoskin (9)
St Peter's RC Primary School, Aberdeen

Thanks Mum

Thanks Mum for everything you've done
Over the past ten years.
For all the time you've shared my joy,
Or wiped away my tiny tears.
It's good to know you're always there for me,
In rain, shine or snow!
You've taught me well in right from wrong,
I hope I'll be like you when I'm older,
I hope you can truly see
How proud I am that you're my mum and I'm
To be your special daughter.
For you mean the whole world to me.

Hayley Lynch (10)
Tanshall Primary School, Glenrothes

Tsunami, 26th December 2004

T is for the terror that hit them on that day
S is for the sadness of the children as they play
U is for unique, the wave that hit the land
N is for the numbers who died upon the sand
A is for them all, the young and the old
M is for the money which is needed, we are told
I is for the innocent people, we could not save because
   On 26th December, came the huge tsunami wave!

Ashleigh Curtis (10)
Tanshall Primary School, Glenrothes

The Caribbean

C is for coral washed up on the shore
A is for always being warm and sunny
R is for rocks, dry and cracked
I is for iguanas on the beach and at the hotel
B is for beach with all its warm sand
B is for breezes at the beach and sea
E is for exciting views from the dry rocks
A is for absolutely the best place to be.
N is for never forgetting the Caribbean.

Liam Baxter (10)
Tanshall Primary School, Glenrothes

Arsenal

A is for Arsene Wenger who manages the team
R is for Reyes who scores the goals
S is for support from all the loyal fans
E is for effort put in by all the players
N is for never giving up, not until the ninetieth minute
A is for all the work done by all of Arsenal
L is for the last minute, the best part of the game.

Ryan Hutton (10)
Tanshall Primary School, Glenrothes

Have You Heard?

Have you ever heard a puff of smoke?
Have you ever heard the green grass grow?
Have you ever heard a spider scream?
Have you ever heard a dream?

Do you hear clouds go by?
Do you hear my brain thinking?
Do you hear a camera flash?
Do you hear my eyes winking?

Have you heard a shooting star?
Have you heard my nose running?
Have you heard the world spin?
Have you heard the flowers grow?
No, these are the sounds of silence.

Kayleigh Finlay (9)
Tanshall Primary School, Glenrothes

Best Friends

B is for buddies
E is for everyday friends
S is for special friends
T is for trouble

F is for friends forever
R is for really funny friends
I is for intelligent friends
E is for especially you
N is for never fight
D is for devils
S is for spectacular friends.

Stacey Gell (11)
Tanshall Primary School, Glenrothes

Springtime

Spring, spring, spring
What would we do without spring?

The blossoms are out,
The tulips are growing in my back garden
What would we do without spring?

The lambs are dancing in the fields
The birds are tweeting in the trees
What would we do without spring?

The days are longer, lighter
The children are out playing
What would we do without spring?

The grass is growing, green as can be,
The sun is out, bright as can be.
What would we do without spring?

Spring is my favourite time of the year,
It's the season that brings new colours and new life.

Without spring there would never be winter,
And more importantly, there would never be any summer!
We could never do without spring.

Stacey Knox (11)
Tanshall Primary School, Glenrothes

Liverpool Football Club

L is for the love of winning cups
I is for intelligent management
V is for vital play
E is for the enjoyment of the game
R is for all the religions that play
P is for the massive pitches which the game is played on
O is for a dreaded own goal
O is for getting caught offside
L is for the love and happiness of a win.

Ryan Watson (10)
Tanshall Primary School, Glenrothes

Disasters

D is for disasters that happen on Earth
I is for ice that makes us feel cold
S is for Sri-Lanka which was hit by the tsunami
A is for acting fast before you're hurt
S is for sand blizzards that happen in the deserts
T is for tornadoes that spin round and round
E is for earthquakes that happen around the world
R is for rain that also causes floods
S is for survivors that have lived through these disasters.

Nadia Mohammed (10)
Tanshall Primary School, Glenrothes

Football

F is for Fernando Ricksen who plays for Rangers
O is for the own goals which are big mistakes
O is for the offside rule
T is for the team that works together
B is for the ball that gets kicked around the pitch
A is for the Annual that comes out every year
L is for the League that they all play in
L is for the love of the crowd that cheer for their teams,
    And for the love of the game.

Steven Neil (10)
Tanshall Primary School, Glenrothes

Rangers Football Club

R is for Rangers, the best team in the Scottish Premier League.
A is for attack, a vital part of the game
N is for Novo, a brilliant player
G is for a goal.
E is for excellent result, when we win,
R is for Rangers who are fantastic to watch,
S is for simply the best!

Philip Gibson (11)
Tanshall Primary School, Glenrothes

Treasure

T is for treasure on the seabed
R is for rubies that are found in the chest
E is for excellent stuff like gold, bronze, silver, purple and red
A is for above the seabed, where the chest is lying
S is for the sea where the chest is, and the shark that guards it!
U is for under the sea where the chest is buried
R is for rubies that sparkle into your eyes
E is for earthquake that takes the chest away . . .

Thomas Lowe (10)
Tanshall Primary School, Glenrothes

The Cough

My cough won't let me work
My cough won't let me walk
My cough won't let me die
My cough won't let me do anything!
My cough won't let me eat
Alas, my cough won't let me play
Well, just let me say, I wish
I didn't cough all the time!
So take a hike cough!

Martin Foy (12)
Tanshall Primary School, Glenrothes

Football

F is for France in the Euro Cup
O is for offside, never a good thing to be
O is for own goal, bad thing it is
T is for Thierry Henry, amazing player
B is for the *crossbar* which we never hit
A is for the Annual that comes out every year
L is for linesman who has a flag to wave
L is for loving it, the game and the team.

Ryan Kelly (10)
Tanshall Primary School, Glenrothes

Spacetacular

Comets speeding round the solar system
like snowballs whizzing past a snowman.

The sun lighting up space
like a light bulb in a dark room.

The planets dangling in the sky
like ornaments hanging from a Christmas tree.

The stars sparkling in the night sky
like glitter on a black page.

Alien spaceships zooming through the sky
like frisbees flying through the park.

Rachel Paterson & Eilidh Bett (11)
Westhill Primary School, Westhill

The Scrambler - Cinquain

Scrambler
Fast and messy
Earth churning, dirt throwing
Adrenaline rushing thriller
Dirt bike.

Euan Dodds & Scott Milne (11)
Westhill Primary School, Westhill

Kennings - What Am I?

Extraterrestrial transportation
Man abductor
Humans distressed
Shiny ship
Space flyer
Super plane

A spaceship.

Ben Little (11)
Westhill Primary School, Westhill

Fear

Fear is like
a monster lurking under the bed.

Fear is like
breathing when the lights are out.

Fear is like
the butcher's knife disappearing from the drawer.

Fear is like
seeing a figure standing in your garden.

Fear is like
someone playing tricks with your mind

Fear is like . . .
Fear itself!

Murray Cruickshank, Diane Fowler & Magnus Warr (11)
Westhill Primary School, Westhill

In Space

A shiny star in the sky
like a candle in a dark room.

The planet Mars, red and dangerous
like a fire burning in space.

A rocky meteorite floating by
like a bottle in the ocean.

A rocket in space
like a pencil on fire, speeding past.

A spaceman on the moon
walks slowly like a sloth.

Euan Duthie & Chris Kerr (11)
Westhill Primary School, Westhill

The Tsunami

The tsunami
Caused by an under sea earthquake
Gigantic, dreadful, rapid
Like a mountain of water
Like a giant made of water, stamping on the land
It makes me feel petrified
Like a spider stuck in a bath
The tsunami
It reminds us of how unpredictable life can be.

Stephanie Clarke & Rona Parkinson (11)
Westhill Primary School, Westhill

Kennings - What Am I?

Wave breaker
Water glider
Air smasher
Wave rider
So fast

The jet ski.

Kirsty MacNeil (11)
Westhill Primary School, Westhill

Space - Cinquain

Spaceship
Shiny and sleek
Flying high in the sky
Whizzing past bright and pretty stars
Rocket.

Jenna Hendry & Kirsty Ogston
Westhill Primary School, Westhill

The Tsunami

The tsunami
A two hundred foot wave
Muscular, devastating, mighty
Like an overpowering machine
Charging against land
Like a curtain of angry water
Saddened by the death of the people
Like a blade of grass waiting to be trampled
The tsunami
Shows us that people are not indestructible.

Cameron Burgess (10) & Abbie Fleming (11)
Westhill Primary School, Westhill

Kennings - What Am I?

Rock shatterer
Earth mover
Tree uplifter
Chair breaker
Ground shaker

The bulldozer.

Natalie Rowley (11)
Westhill Primary School, Westhill

Kennings - What Am I?

Water dancer
Wave surfer
Party goer
Wind catcher
Elegant lady

The yacht.

Laurie Stuart (11)
Westhill Primary School, Westhill

The Tsunami

Two hundred feet in size
Devastating, horrific, unexpected
Like a rampaging water rhino
Stampeding towards land
Like a train on full speed,
I feel there is nothing I can do
I feel as helpless as a strand of grass
The tsunami
It reminds me how lucky I am.

Calum Ritchie & Alastair Forsyth (11)
Westhill Primary School, Westhill

Tsunami

The tsunami
Triggered by a seabed eruption
Powerful, destructive, devastating
Like the sea, invading the beach
Like a tiger, pouncing on its prey
It makes me feel distressed and alone
Like a single grain of sand
The tsunami
Makes you understand how important life is.

Amber Wynn & Nicole Anderson (10)
Westhill Primary School, Westhill

Combine Harvester - Cinquain

Combine
Food harvester
Wheat crusher, big mower
Helping the farmer feed the world
Shredder.

Jack Davidson & Elliott Pettitt (11)
Westhill Primary School, Westhill

Black Car

(Nursery rhyme on the theme of transport based on 'Twinkle! Twinkle! Little Star')

Brum, brum black car
Chomping on the fuel
Eating, eating till you're nearly full
Open up the garage door
We'll go out to get some more
Chomping, chomping on the fuel
Come on now! You must be full!

Molly Bedrock & Tabatha Wright (10)
Westhill Primary School, Westhill

Tsunami

The tsunami
Gigantic wall of water
Deadly, dangerous, powerful
Like the sea attacking the land
Like an underwater meteor blowing up the Earth
It makes me feel terrified
Like someone about to be stung by a million jellyfish.

The tsunami
Reminds us to be thankful for all we've got.

Paul Sheach, Jinu Jang & Sean Cowie (10)
Westhill Primary School, Westhill

The Tsunami

A devastating wave
Destroying, terrifying, destructive
Like a big mouth swallowing the land
Like a mythical sea god devouring the sea
I feel helpless for the survivors that are ill and weak
Like a wave of sadness has hit me
The tsunami
Reminds me how important life is.

Ailsa Collie & Nia McKain
Westhill Primary School, Westhill

The Tsunami

An underwater earthquake gave birth to it
Powerful, aggressive, destructive
Like a sea army that cannot be defeated
Like a barrier of surging water
It makes me feel small
Like a grain of sand lying on the beach
The tsunami
Can sweep away our loved ones.

Zakary Rothwell & Gillian Wright (10)
Westhill Primary School, Westhill

The Tsunami

The tsunami
The biggest disaster ever, an underwater earthquake
Appalling, severe, distressing
Like a sea monster devouring the beach
Like a bulldozer made by the sea
I feel helpless wanting to help
Like a stranded fish stuck on the shore
The tsunami
Reminds us how fortunate we are.

David Ross Mackenzie & Kyle Johannesson (11)
Westhill Primary School, Westhill

The Tsunami

Made by an underwater earthquake
Gigantic, incredible, rare
Like an avalanche of water
Like a racing car
It makes me feel tiny
Like a tiny pebble lost in the ocean
The tsunami
Reminds me how lucky I am.

Stephanie Allard & Jack Grimmer (11)
Westhill Primary School, Westhill

The School

Our school is the noisiest and worst school in the world.
My classroom is as noisy as a disco with its music blaring
And the toilets smell like animal dung!
Some children swing across the class like Tarzan in the jungle,
Whilst others run round like cheetahs, catching their prey.
But there's always a kid in the corner, screaming like
A gorilla protecting its baby.
And then finally there's the teacher.
Trying to control the children like a zoo manager
Getting the animals to calm down,
And now you know why our school is the noisiest
And worst school in the world . . . *only kidding!*

Graham Repper (10)
Westhill Primary School, Westhill

The Tsunami

The tsunami
Built up from an undersea earthquake
Powerful, strong, determined
Like a wall of water.
Like a sea monster racing inland
It makes me feel helpless
Like a tiny grain of sand that nobody notices
The tsunami
Reminds me how quickly life can be changed.

Kirsty Gollifer (10) & Johanna Goldie (11)
Westhill Primary School, Westhill

Transport - Haiku

The plane wouldn't start
This puzzled the mechanics
But it had no fuel!

Stuart Duncan (11)
Westhill Primary School, Westhill

Cars! Cars! Cars!

Big cars,
Fast cars.
Tiny little mini cars,
Long sleek limo cars.
I have seen a few.

Sports cars,
Vintage cars.
Shiny bright new cars,
Formula One racing cars.
Make me happy too.

Panda cars,
Beetle cars.
4x4 Rally cars.
Last of all, best of all -
I love Ferrari cars!

Jordan Stevely (11)
Woodlands Primary School, Irvine

Scotland's The Best

The place I live in
Is none other than Scotland.
My favourite place in the world.
Where I don't need to be jumbled
Is Scotland.

It's not the best weather,
But I can stand the heather
And when I need a rest
Scotland's the best.

Ruth Dempster (8)
Woodlands Primary School, Irvine

Bags! Bags! Bags!

Blue bags,
Pink bags.
Small, sparkly, black bags.
Big, bright, multicoloured bags,
And there's more to come.

Silk bags,
Leather bags.
White furry animal bags,
Huge yellow rucksack bags.
Don't forget the camping bags.

Bin bags,
Plastic bags.
One big holiday bag.
Last of all, best of all
My big blue school bag.

Katie Bell (11)
Woodlands Primary School, Irvine

Hands

Pink hands can touch paper,
Ice hands can freeze to death.
Strong hands can do Karate,
Girl's hands can dance.
Boy's hands can play basketball,
Long hands can stretch.
Teacher's hands can care for you,
Mum's hands can cuddle you,
My hands can tickle people!

Ashley Donaghy (8)
Woodlands Primary School, Irvine

Memories

One, little face and a pink dummy tit,
Two, green eyes that always sparkled.
Three, starting nursery, I was so excited.
Four, doing my first cartwheel - quite intense.
Five, having a tantrum and throwing custard at the wall.
Six, went to Jed Moore's birthday party - bouncy, bouncy.
Seven, doing my first wall climb at Blackpool.
Eight, went to Tenerife, got hit full face by a small tidal wave.
Nine, my dad having gout, he was quite ill.
Ten, my birthday party at the Thistle Hotel. Splashing!
Eleven, having fun at Blackpool on the Irn-Bru revolution.

Kerri-Ann Murdoch (11)
Woodlands Primary School, Irvine

What Is Your Wish?

I wish I were an animator to make a cool cartoon,
I wish I could find a new planet and call it Derrizoon,
I wish I had a solid gold loo that shone in the light,
I wish I had a super jumping kangaroo that could send me a flight.
I wish I was a basketball player to play in a tournament,
I wish I had a band, I would call it Metal Dent.

Hari Edwin (8)
Woodlands Primary School, Irvine

What Is Your Wish?

I wish I was a mermaid swimming in the sea,
I wish I was a better ballet dancer, so I could go
                              right up on my tiptoes,
I wish I could have a bigger house on the beach,
I wish I was a gymnast to walk across a tightrope.

Shannon Ward (8)
Woodlands Primary School, Irvine

What Is Your Wish?

I wish I was a gymnast doing lots of fancy flips and somersaults,
I wish I had a shop so I never had to pay.
I wish I had a palace and I'd dust it all day,
I wish my dad's leg would get better, so we would have
lots of time to play.
I wish I was an artist drawing some fancy drawings,
I wish I was a bear so I could have very long claws.
I wish that I could fly so I could see the view.

Ashley Lawson (8)
Woodlands Primary School, Irvine

Dolls! Dolls! Dolls!

Girl dolls,
Boy dolls,
Very fragile China dolls.
Pretty little princess dolls,
Those are just a few.

Barbie dolls,
Cindy dolls.
Crying, talking baby dolls.
Big dolls, small dolls,
Funky fairy dolls too.

Black dolls,
White dolls,
Don't forget the Russian dolls.
Last of all, best of all,
I like Bratz dolls.

Katie Tasker (11)
Woodlands Primary School, Irvine